"Mark's imagination, like the God about whom he writes, is dangerously unpredictable. The Holy Wild is a gateway to the spiritual world that many of us forget exists. His treatment of the Good Samaritan alone is worth the read."

JOHN ORTBERG,
Author of *Everybody's Normal Till You Get to Know Them*

"He's done it again. The Holy Wild is a fabulous book. I want to write like Mark when I grow up."

BETH MOORE,
Founder of Living Proof Ministries

MARK BUCHANAN

THE HOLY WILD

MULTNOMAH
BOOKS

THE HOLY WILD

Published in association with the literary agency of Ann Spangler and Company,
1420 Pontiac Road SE, Grand Rapids, Michigan 49506.

International Standard Book Number: 978-1-59052-448-0

Cover image of mountains by Photonica / Jason Frank Rothenberg
Background cover image by Photolibrary.com
Interior design by Katherine Lloyd, The DESK, Bend, Oregon

Unless otherwise indicated, Scripture quotations are from:
The Holy Bible, New International Version © 1973, 1984 by
International Bible Society, used by permission of Zondervan Publishing House.

Other Scripture quotations are from:
The Amplified Bible (AMP) © 1965, 1987
by Zondervan Publishing House.

The Message by Eugene H. Peterson
© 1993, 1994, 1995, 1996, 2000, 2001, 2002.
Used by permission of NavPress Publishing Group.
All rights reserved.

The Holy Bible, New King James Version (NKJV) © 1984 by Thomas Nelson, Inc.

Published in the United States by Multnomah, an imprint of the Crown Publishing Group,
a division of Penguin Random House LLC, New York.

MULTNOMAH® and its moutain colophon are registered trademarks
of Penguin Random House LLC.

Library of Congress Cataloging-in-Publication Data
Buchanan, Mark Aldham.
   The holy wild / by Mark Buchanan.
         p. cm.
Includes bibliographical references.
   ISBN 1-59052-249-4
         1-59052-448-9
   1. Trust in God--Christianity. I. Title
   BV4637.B83 2003
   231'.6--dc22

2003014193

I dedicate this book to my church,
New Life Community Baptist.
I've never known a people as peculiar as you.
May we dwell long together in the Holy Wild.

CONTENTS

ACKNOWLEDGMENTS

Since God did not give me the gifts of a monk, he made me a monk's failed cousin, a writer. Both callings render you slightly odd, a man alone in a room, denying one part of his manhood in order to awaken another. Both force you to shape silence and darkness and waiting into prayer. Both teach you the agonies of silence and of speaking, and the way God's voice can brim in each. Both require you to listen much, pray much, study much, plow much. One demands you drink much wine, the other much coffee. I'll let you figure out which is which.

Both are lonely vocations.

But even monks and writers have their community, those whose patience and generosity make our quixotic and somewhat leechy existence possible, even profitable. My community is huge, the living and the dead, a great cloud of witnesses. You are too many to name all at once. But at the risk of missing many, I dare name a few.

My church. How amazing you are—how gifted and giving and forgiving and peculiar, in the best way. You keep teaching me, over and over, how to dance in the Holy Wild, going headlong into a dangerous obedience and discovering life there. Thank you.

My publisher. How gracious you are—how encouraging and strengthening and shrewd, in the best way. You keep pushing me, again and again, to map the Holy Wild, to name its depths and heights, to trace its outer reaches and inner sanctums. Thank you. Thanks especially to Bill Jensen for continuing to champion me, and to my editor Heather Kopp (and David) for disentangling—or when all else failed, slicing clean through—many of the early manuscript's Gordian knots and weaving it back into wholeness. And thanks, Heather, for great chapter titles.

My agent, Ann Spangler. How wise you are—how discerning and supportive and feisty, in the best way. You keep averting me, time after time, from pitfalls I'm headed toward in my sometimes reckless pursuit of the Holy Wild. Thank you.

My family. How loving you are—how welcoming and protective and ordinary, in the best way. You keep bringing me, day after day, to the reality of the Holy Wild, right here, right now, in the simple and mundane things—bread, water, jumping on the trampoline, lying beside you in bed, talking in whispers. I love you, Cheryl, Adam, Sarah, and Nicola. Thank you.

My God. How—well, that's what this book is about. Thank You.

To Him be all glory.

MAPPING THE HOLY WILD

I 'm tired.

I bet you are, too. Weariness is epidemic, a virus we've carried in our blood so long, so deep, we're almost immune to it, like those people in tropical lands who are chronically malarial. If you're like me, you've pretty much adapted to it—your manic spurts and sluggish spells, your outbursts and breakdowns, your jangled nerves and leaden limbs. Your *restlessness*. All the things to do. A dozen fire sticks to juggle, a hundred dike holes to plug, a thousand cats to herd. All the whirring, whirling, wearying busyness of life.

It makes you tired.

I hope God loves irony. Because I set out to write a book on resting, resting in God, resting in His rich, varied, steady character. And then partway through, I got so rushed and panicky—so tired—I began to write out of my own anxiety. I wanted to describe life from the eyes of Mary, the one who sits in rapturous wonder at Jesus' feet, drinking it all in, but found myself inside the skin of Martha, the meddling, fiddling, fuming sister who resents both Jesus and anyone who gets close to Him—and spewing it all out. She's the one who won't rest and so wants to spoil it for the rest.

She knows nothing of the Holy Wild.

But one of the gifts of writing is that it forces you to take your subject seriously. I think that, in my case anyhow, God calls me to write the books I am the least qualified to write. The reason is as obvious as it is trite: Before I can teach it, I must first learn it.

I wrote this book during what was easily the busiest of my forty-two years. And yet, except for my Martha moments, I have *lived* this year—entering into its desolations and consolations—more fully than any I can remember.

I have learned to rest more in God. And I have tasted more of God.

This book is about that God. It is about leaning all the way into Him, learning to put our entire weight in who He is and what He does. And it's about discovering life as God always meant it to be.

"Come to me," Jesus said, "all who are weary and burdened, and I will give you rest." That is not an invitation to idleness. He doesn't want to lull you to sleep. He wants to awaken you. He wants to make you fully alive.

He wants to take you on the ride of your life, into the Holy Wild.

Shalom,
Mark Buchanan
June 2003

Part I

Drink from This Stream

How God's Benevolent Nature
Sustains Us in Trouble and Suffering

Chapter One

THE GOD OF
THE HOLY WILD

The summer I wrote this, we discovered a nest of snakes living in our house. It was a hot spell, and often we retreated to the basement to escape the worst of it.

We weren't the only ones, it turned out.

A mother snake, at some point, had found her way into our house (we left most of our doors open that summer to create airflow). She had slithered into the back corner of the coolest, most interior room, and there hatched a brood of baby snakes: tiny black serpents, with slender, tapered bodies and teardrop-shaped heads and little, red flickering tongues.

I hate snakes. I once heard about a man who, digging in his garden, hacked his shin apart with his spade when a garter snake slithered up his pant leg. I understood this: the panic, the wildness, the madness, the willingness to maim yourself to protect yourself. If it had been me and not Adam and Eve in Eden, we wouldn't be in the trouble we're in, but not because I have greater virtue; simply because it was a *serpent* who seduced them. I'd have killed it first.

One evening I came home from a deacons' meeting (was this itself a sign?) and Cheryl, wide-eyed and pale, met me at the door. "We have snakes," she said, hissing and writhing, snakelike, herself. She and my son had already managed to capture in a jar two of the babies. It was my job, I was told, to track down the mother. I began with stiff caution, jabbing sticks under furniture then leaping back, expecting Medusa's head to come shaking out at me. Everything I rousted out—a wisp of dust, a stray hairpin, a snip of thread—startled me. Every sensation of something touching me—the edge of a quilt brushing my shin, the corner of a desk biting my hip, a strand of cobweb trailing across my neck, the frays of cut cloth tickling my arm—sent me into a spasm of thrashing. After a while, I got more bold, more determined, especially since I had looked everywhere and found nothing.

"She's gone," I said. "Must have got out somehow. She's a bad mother. Abandoned the little ones to their fate. Imagine that."

Cheryl wasn't buying it. "Check again," she said. "Take a better look under the hide-a-bed. Mark, I spend hours in this room every week. My parents are coming on Monday to sleep in this room. I won't rest until I know it's safe."

So I pulled the mattress off the hide-a-bed and poked my head under the frame.

Bingo.

There she was, curled up on the back ledge of the bed frame. She was only about fourteen inches long and no thicker than my baby finger. But in my phobic, manic alertness, she may as well have been a Burmese python, smugly swallowing the dog, just getting started.

What followed was ten minutes of slapstick comedy—a burlesque of blundering, scrambling antics, a wild pantomime of overreaction. I chased that snake around, trying to pinch its thin, wriggling body between two blunt-end four-foot sticks and drop it in a small-mouthed jar. It kept getting free, to the accompaniment of our shrieks and hollers, and would scoot off to another corner and pile its body into dense coils. After several tries, it was glaringly obvious this approach was futile. I asked my son to fetch my garden gloves. I would have to pick it up.

I did it. There was no heroism or elegance in it. I held the snake away from me like I might a dead fish that had been left out in the sun. But I did it.

Over the next few days, as we found more snakes, we discovered that our nine-year-old daughter Sarah was fearless with them. She would simply pick each snake up with her bare hands, hold it near her face, scold it as though it were a naughty dog who chewed up the hose, then set it loose in the garden, telling it to go find its mother.

Here's the thing. Ever since, it's been hard for me to rest in that room. Walking into it, I slow, halt, turn, look now this way, now that. I even look up, as though I'm dealing with a fat, hungry tree snake, its body languidly draped along the curtain rod, its head undulating downward. Every nerve in me is heightened, every muscle taut and trembling, and the little hairs on my arms stand up.

I may never sleep in that bed again. After we found the snakes, we had a string of stifling hot nights—nights like huge furnaces, roaring and devouring, the surface of things glazed with heat. Nights that skewered and roasted you like a pig on a spit, turning slow, dripping, shriveling. On nights like those, we used to escape to the coolness of the basement to sleep.

But no more.

Instead, we now suffer upstairs, suffer all night long. There we lie, listless and restless, prickly and sweaty, longing for relief. On the worst of these nights I almost give in, slip downstairs, open the hide-a-bed, and crawl in. But I know it's no good. Every time I shut my eyes, I would see them, thousands of them, every length and thickness of them, twining, coiling, darting, hissing, squirming. I know that if I ever got to sleep's threshold, to that blissful, hypnotic place where your body hovers over oblivion and starts to ease down, something would graze the nape of my neck or tickle the hollow in my collarbone, and I would leap up, wild with panic, punching the air and slapping myself.

I don't trust that bed.

THE FUNNY THING IS, the bed hasn't changed at all. It's just as sturdy, just as comfortable. It can hold my weight, soothe my soreness. What has changed is my experience. I now harbor a suspicion that dread things lurk beneath. And so I approach the bed with a guardedness that I won't let drop.

This book is about resting in the character of God. I take it to be that resting and trusting are near synonyms: I rest where I can trust. I rest on the bed that I'm assured won't buckle beneath my weight, in the room where I'm confident I won't be left vulnerable to enemies or predators, in the house where I'm certain I won't be exposed to toxins or contagions. If I doubt any of these things, if I lack trust, I may sleep in the house or the room or the bed—but I won't really *rest* there. I'll do it out of sheer exhaustion, maybe, but not out of trust. I'll be fitful and anxious, always checking my back, tense and clenching, a hair trigger on my reflexes.

My point: *How I think about the bed determines whether or not I rest in it.* The bed, as I said, hasn't changed. But I have.

Sometimes our faith in God is like that: snake-infested. God doesn't change, but how we think about Him does. Dread things, we suspect, lurk in the basement. It is hard for us to rest in God, because it is hard for us to trust.

❧ ❧ ❧

MY FIRST BOOK WAS called *Your God Is Too Safe.* In it, I invited us to be done with the god of our own invention, the god who resembles a museum curator, pale, quibbling, fastidious; or a group therapist, vague, earnest, doting; but not the Lion of Judah, fierce and wild and good. I diagnosed our inner stuckness as a mostly theological sickness, an impaired vision of God as God. For various reasons, we would rather contrive a god who is perfectly content to make his bed in the servants' quarters than worship the God who is on the loose, ruling from the heights, slipping in among the ranks, skulking about in disguise, equally absent and present in most disruptive ways. Then I prescribed a way out: the practice of holy habits. These are disciplines that, like well-treasured and well-guarded family recipes, have been passed along from generation to generation among Christians. They are simple, adaptable, workable, and they train us in a steadiness toward God, "a long obedience in the same direction."[1]

I coined two terms in that book. The first one, *borderland,* describes the condition of stuckness—a conversion without regeneration, an initial encounter with Jesus that doesn't lead to a life abiding with Jesus. It's an acquaintanceship devoid of intimacy, dependency, obedience. People on borderland have grown comfortable with boredom. They have settled for a God "on call," a God available for crises and fiascos, who does a bit of juggling with weather patterns and parking stalls but who otherwise remains unobtrusive as a chambermaid, tidying things up while you're at brunch, leaving a crisp sash of tissue around the lid of the toilet bowl to let you know all is in order. The problem, obviously, is that this god—so kind, so shy, so tame—has nothing whatsoever to do with the God of the Bible. This god resembles not even remotely the God whose Spirit broods and dances, the God who topples entire empires, sometimes overnight, the God who reveals himself in the Christ who looks big men in the eye and says, "Follow me," and then walks away, not waiting for a reply. The God who calls us off borderland.

The other term, *the Holy Wild,* describes life with the God who is. The Holy Wild is what life, drunk to the lees, lived to the hilt, is like—life where we walk with the God who is surprising, dangerous, mysterious, alongside us though we fail to recognize Him, then disappearing the minute we do. It is the terrain where God doesn't always make sense of our sad or bland lives, our calamities and banalities, but who keeps meeting us in the thick and thin of those lives.

In *Your God Is Too Safe,* I used the famous story from *The Lion, the Witch and the Wardrobe,* the most famous book of C. S. Lewis's most famous work, the Chronicles of Narnia. This is the story where Mr. Beaver, in response to Lucy's question of whether the great lion Aslan is "quite safe," explodes,

"Safe? Safe? Who said anything about safe? Of course he isn't safe. But he's good."

It's a great scene. But equally great, and lesser known, is the scene from the Narnia adventure *The Silver Chair*. A haughty girl named Jill Pole lands in Narnia with Eustace Scrubb—once a spoiled and whiny child who, in an earlier visit to Narnia, experienced an agonizing but transforming encounter with Aslan. Jill gets into a tussle with Eustace at a cliff's edge, and she ends up pushing him off. As Eustace falls, Aslan rushes up and blows a huge stream of breath to catch Eustace and, magic-carpet-like, carry him far, far away, to safety—and to danger.

Aslan then turns and, to Jill's relief, walks away into the forest.

But she grows thirsty. She can hear from within the forest the sound of a stream. Her thirst finally drives her to seek the source of this sound. She proceeds cautiously, afraid. She soon discovers the stream but is paralyzed by what she sees there: Aslan, huge and golden, still as a statue but terribly alive, sitting beside the water. She waits for a long time, wrestling with her thoughts, hoping he will go away. Aslan finally speaks: "If you are thirsty, you may drink." Jill is startled by this and holds back.

"Are you not thirsty?" said the Lion.

"I am *dying* of thirst," said Jill.

"Then drink," said the Lion.

"May I—could I—would you mind going away while I do?" said Jill.

The Lion answered this only by a look and a very low growl. And just as Jill gazed at its motionless bulk, she realized that she might as well have asked the whole mountain to move aside for her convenience.

The delicious rippling noise of the stream was driving her near frantic.

"Will you promise not to—do anything to me, if I come?"

"I make no promise," said the Lion.

Jill was so thirsty now that, without noticing it, she had come a step nearer.

"*Do* you eat girls?" she said.

"I have swallowed up girls and boys, women and men, kings and emperors, cities and realms," said the Lion. It didn't say this as if it were boasting, nor as if it were sorry, nor as if it were angry. It just said it.

"I daren't come and drink," said Jill.

"Then you will die of thirst," said the Lion.

"Oh dear!" said Jill, coming another step nearer. "I suppose I must go and look for another stream then."

"There is no other stream," said the Lion.[2]

That is where this book—my third—comes in: *There is no other stream.* This is about living in the Holy Wild, living with this God who, without apology, without anger, without boast, swallows up girls and boys, women and men, kings and emperors, cities and realms.

The God who gives us no options. Either we drink from this stream, or we die.

ৼ ৼ ৼ

WHICH RAISES THE QUESTION I really want to ask. Jill's question. My question. Maybe yours, too.

Can God be trusted?

Is there no other stream? If I turn my back on the Lion to drink, will He leave me unmolested? If He swallows me, then what?

Is the character of God such that we can both *risk* for Him and *rest* in Him?

I have set out to write about resting in the character of God: learning to put all our weight—the fullness of who we are, what we dream, the things we cherish—in the fullness of who God is. To sing beneath the shadows of His wings. To pour ourselves out like a drink offering for Him. My conviction is that, unless and until we rest in God, we'll never risk for God. We will at most skirt the edges of the Holy Wild but never venture in, and probably not even that much. We will sit by the stream all day, dying of thirst but not daring to bend to drink. We will toss in our bed all night, dying of heat but not daring to crawl beneath the cool sheets waiting downstairs.

If I truly desire the Holy Wild—living face-to-face with the beautiful, dangerous God, not safe but good—I need to know who this God is. I need to know Him, more and more, deeper and deeper, with biblical clarity. To know Him in my head and in my creeds but also—with King David's instincts—in my guts and in my bones.

If I am to go anywhere with God, to follow Him, by hook or by crook, staggering, leaping, dancing, crawling, all the way into the Holy Wild, I need more than a textbook knowledge of Him. I need more than piety, more than erudition, more than good intentions.

I need to drink and drink from the stream, even if it means—especially if it means—getting swallowed up.

ℐ ℐ ℐ

MANY OF US ARE confessional giants but ethical midgets. We talk a big game. We profess the highest, purest orthodoxy. Our creed is impeccable. "God is," we begin, and what follows could pass muster before the most rigorous theological council or inquisition.

But then the trouble starts. God is...what?

"What comes into our minds when we think about God,"

A. W. Tozer wrote in *The Knowledge of the Holy*, "is the most important thing about us."[3]

What comes into our minds when we think about God is the most important thing about us.

Not that any one of us can have a full understanding of God. Saint Augustine walked the seashore one day, pondering the majesty of God. He saw a small boy who had dug a hole in the sand. The boy kept scooting down to the ocean, scooping up water in a seashell, and scrambling back to pour the water in the hole.

"What are you doing?" Augustine asked him.

"I'm going to pour the sea into that hole," the boy said.

Ah, Augustine thought. *That is what I have been trying to do. Standing at the ocean of infinity, I have tried to grasp it with my finite mind.*[4]

Sometimes theology is sheer hubris—a boy with a seashell trying to gather the ocean. And yet, we need it, theology.

Theology is our attempt to render God through creed and dogma, through words we have handpicked, weighed, time-tested. Words that saints and sages, kings and rag pickers, scholars and schoolboys, have treasured, fondled, squandered, squabbled over, mocked, ignored, refurbished, worn smooth from use. Words like *holy relics,* which we adore in simple piety, or smash in prophetic rage.

We need these words, these creeds, this dogma. We need theology.

But that's not the end of it. To have a carefully tested theology is good, but it's not the same thing as *knowing* God. Too often theology ends shy of love, worship, service. Too often it gets stuck in smugness, dryness, rigidity. Too often it is as impersonal as calculus. Too often it is *mere* words.

Jesus' apostles were pretty much doctrinal flunkies, blunder-prone, befuddled, cotton-mouthed with folly. Meanwhile, demons almost always showed themselves to be astute theologians.

A man who was possessed by an evil spirit cried out to Jesus, "*I know who you are—the Holy One of God!*"[5]

"What do you want with me, *Jesus, Son of the Most High God?*" the demon-thronged Legion asked.[6]

In Ephesus, a demon-possessed girl followed Paul and Silas, shouting after them, "These men are *servants of the Most High God, who are telling you the way to be saved.*"[7]

James summed it up this way: "You believe that there is one God. Good! Even the demons believe that—and shudder."[8]

What marks Jesus' disciples from His enemies is not theological acumen; His enemies often had the edge there. It's this: Disciples follow Him, bewildered as they often are, while enemies oppose Him, clear-minded though they be.

I want to make disciples. So I want the knowledge of God to increase. But I also want the love of God to grow stronger, to enrich our theology but, even more, our worship. To sharpen our talk about God, but precisely so that we talk more to God.

To enlarge our understanding of His ways, but solely so that we walk in them, steady, unswerving, not growing weary.

I will have failed if God is named but not praised, analyzed but not glorified, seen but not sought. I will have failed if we know better the character of God but are no more inclined than before to rest in Him. And if we don't rest in Him, we'll never risk for Him.

This book is about what it means to know God so thoroughly that we rest in Him totally and, therefore, are willing to risk for Him completely. It's about entering the Holy Wild by way of deepest intimacy with the Holy God. I want to be able to face the snakes beneath my bed like my daughter Sarah did: calm, amused, unafraid, and able to return afterward to that bed—that perfectly good bed—to lie full on it and rest.

In the following chapters, we will look at the character of God—God's uniqueness, His justice, His mercy, His creativity, His wisdom, His playfulness, His suffering, His everlastingness, and more. Some of these characteristics you've likely read about, pondered, heard sermons about, maybe even preached some yourself.

Others, maybe not. I've seen or heard very little on the playfulness of God—the childlike God, singing and dancing, relishing the sheer riotous abundance of colors and shapes and sounds.

So we'll look at the character of God, but this is not a book on doctrine or divine attributes. Such books are useful, but plentiful. Rather, this is an attempt to explore one large question: *What does it mean to know God so well that we trust God no matter what?*

What does it mean to rest in the character of God? If God is playful, what does it mean for me to enter into that? If He is just, what does it mean to trust in that? If He is creative, what does it mean to imitate that?

This book is about entering the Holy Wild by way of deepest intimacy.

THERE IS A SCENE in the first *Lord of the Rings* movie where the fellowship of travelers must enter the ancient mines of Moria for a perilous but ultimately redemptive journey. It is their one and only way through the treacherous mountains to safe haven. It's a journey into the Holy Wild.

Only, the huge stone doors leading into the mines are sealed shut. Over the arch of the door is written, in Elvish, this inscription:

The Doors of Durin, Lord of Moria.
Speak friend and enter.

The hobbit Merry asks the de facto leader of the party, the wise and ancient Gandalf, what this means. "It's quite simple," he says. "If you're a friend, you speak the password and the doors will open." Gandalf musters his powers and in his deepest and most solemn voice utters some ancient incantation.

Nothing.

He speaks again, with commanding authority.

Nothing.

He pushes against the door. He shouts. He gets angry.

Nothing.

Hours later, they're all still there, bored and anxious, Gandalf muttering away. The door hasn't budged. Gandalf sits down, his back to the door, weary, defeated. Frodo the hobbit looks up and reads the inscription once again: "Speak friend and enter."

"It's a riddle," he says. "Gandalf, what is the Elvish word for *friend*?"

Gandalf looks at him, puzzled, annoyed.

"*Mellon*," he says.

And with the uttering of that one word, the door swings open.[9]

Sometimes we try so hard. We push, we shove, we shout, we declare, we say every prayer we know. And all we do is wear ourselves out.

When all God intends is for us to speak *friend* and enter.

Chapter Two

EULOGY FOR A GIANT

God's Goodness

Some people seem born for bad luck. Wide, soft targets for catastrophe, epic fall guys, cosmic stooges. All they touch shatters or withers. They breathe blight. Their timing—in sports, in stocks, in real estate, in relationships, in life—chronically misfires. Lawsuits, bankruptcies, bad news, hardships, sickness, disasters— all these find them with cruel, unerring accuracy and numbing frequency, as though trouble is rigged with a homing device calibrated just for them and aimed straight at their vital organs.

Like Roger. Roger can't win. If something ever seemed to turn out right for him, it was no more than a setup, a sting operation, a greater height from which to fall. After a bleak stretch of unemployment, Roger gets a good job, only to lose it two days before Christmas just after taking out a massive car loan. If he buys a house, the next week the market tanks and Roger discovers dry rot in the attic and mold in the cellar. Roger misses planes. He loses credit cards. He makes wrong turns. He gets audited. He falls deathly ill the night before his long-awaited vacation to Cancun and has to cancel (but he neglected to get insurance for that).

And those are the minor things, the mere mishaps and pratfalls, the comedy of errors. The slapstick. There are other things—dark, rotted, crooked things—that plague him and taunt him. A terror and a sadness stalk him. He is a haunted man, a fugitive from tragedy.

You know a Roger. Most of us do. They're good men. They're honorable. They're honest. They do right by their families. They mean well. They work hard. And yet, it seems, God has chosen them only to punish them, to gloat over or, worse, yawn at their misfortune. God has elected them, on a whim maybe, or a wager, or a dare, to suffer Jobian trials. And He gives the devil a free hand to pummel and plunder while He stands back, mildly curious to see how it all turns out.

Or so it seems.

We know a Roger, and we also know a Lacey. For her, life has always worked. Blessing follows obedience. Good things bloom from good deeds. She's pretty, smart, gracious, vivacious. She has a knack for getting things right and never had cause to doubt that God works all things together for good for people like her. She hasn't even had to take that on faith. That's been her ever-present experience, a vivid empirical reality she could no more deny than the grass beneath her feet, a piece of logic so watertight it could be a law of nature.

Until one day. One long, dark day, when all that *can* break—break down, break apart, break loose—does break.

A car accident that snatches away her husband and three children and leaves her for the rest of her life spindly-limbed and motionless, breathing from a tube, bound to a wheelchair.

Or a stalker who abducts her five-year-old boy in the park on a lovely summer day, snatching him from her life forever.

Or a revelation about her husband—the man she loves, the father of her children, her high school sweetheart—that is horrifying and bizarre, the stuff of cheap melodrama, so outlandish that it's ridiculous, but that proves true.

One moment that changes everything. One moment that can't be undone, can't be contained, can't be accounted for, that demolishes in a single instant an entire lifetime of good moments.

And either way, Roger or Lacey, it makes you wonder, *Is God good?*

᚛ ᚛ ᚛

YOU'VE ASKED IT. Even if you've never voiced the question out loud, you've felt its grip, its bite, its leer.

When you want something desperately, and God says, "No." When you dread something deeply, and God says, "So?"

When, like Moses, you would be content to spend the rest of your days tending grazing sheep in the wilds, and God says, "Go to the palace now and confront Pharaoh." When, like Nehemiah, you would be pleased to end your days in the palace, serving—and tasting!—wine and delicacies for the king, and God says, "Go to the ghetto now and restore its ruins."

Is God good? Does He care for *me?*

If I turn my back on the Lion to drink, will He guard me or rend me?

Since this is a book on the character of God—the trustworthiness of God—goodness is a good place to start. The God of the Holy Wild: We know He's not safe, *but is He good?*

Jesus' parable about the talents is really a story about this. The man who buries his talent sees the master as a hard man, reaping what he never sowed, demanding what he refused to provide. He sees him as a taker, not a giver. A miser, a taskmaster, a Scrooge. The Sheriff of Nottingham, he is, deficient in goodness.

This is where the shoe pinches. Lurking behind much of our thinking about God is suspicion on exactly this point. If I ask for bread, will He give me a stone? If I ask for a fish, will He give me a snake? I know I'm not to put Him to the test and *leap* from the temple; but if I stumble at its edge, will He keep me from falling? Will His angels catch me, or will He watch me hit and crumple on the stones below? If I turn to drink, will He pounce? Or maybe worse, just watch as some hungry beast stalks and overpowers and devours me?

A man I know who has traversed many seasons of pain said to me recently, "God sometimes seems like that neighbor who keeps borrowing your stuff and either forgetting to return it or bringing it back damaged, with no explanation. You wonder how much more of your stuff you'll entrust to him."

Is He good?

The question is ancient. We have asked it from the beginning. Adam and Eve asked it—or let the serpent ask it for them—and decided the answer was no. Job, in a torment of physical and emotional agony, asked it and got rebuked for demanding answers to things too great for his understanding. David asked it and wrote psalms like Magellan sketched maps, like Leibniz and Newton devised calculus, like Heinrich Schliemann unearthed Troy's ruins—trying to give shape to the vastness and intricacy and mystery that sprawled out before him. Jeremiah, brooding over a doomed nation, lamenting over a desolate city, asked the question. Some of the apostle Paul's confessions (and the sheer scrappy vigor of his apologetics) suggest he asked it, too.

But maybe in all Scripture no one asked it with the blunt grief and sharp anger of the prophet Habakkuk. "How long, O LORD, must I call for help, but you do not listen?" These are his opening words. He continues, "[How long do I] cry out to you, 'Violence!' but you do not save?" Habakkuk's complaint goes on from here, accusation piled on grievance, all of it pungent with the prophet's indignation, his gruff impatience with pat answers and pious euphemisms. He stews with anger, bristles with bitterness. He stands God down and refuses to budge until the Almighty comes clean.

And God answers. But it's an answer stunning in its illogic, shocking in its impiety: God is raising up the Babylonians, that "ruthless and impetuous people" who are "feared and dreaded...a law to themselves...[who] come bent on violence...guilty men, whose own strength is their god."[1] God is raising them up to execute His justice. God is raising them up to punish the evil rampant in Israel.

For Habakkuk, this is no answer at all. How could He? How dare He? Why would God, the holy One whose "eyes are too pure to look on evil," who "cannot tolerate wrong"[2]— why would God use the godless to carry out His purposes? The Babylonians are predators, pillagers, maulers, idolaters. They worship wood and stone. They glory in their own raw physicality, their own surliness and brawn, their own power to crush and rend. Their very existence mocks heaven.

Habakkuk's complaint, at root, is this: God betrays Himself. By using the Babylonians as instruments of His purpose, God violates His own character. He mocks everything He's taught us to believe about Him—His fairness, His faithfulness, His mercy, His purity.

His goodness.

Can He be trusted? Is there no other stream? If I turn my

back on this God, will He guard me or rend me?

Who can trust a God who seems Machiavellian in His plots, capricious in His devices, who resorts to the expedient at the cost of the good, who consorts with evildoers? A God who, contrary to the depiction of the righteous man in Psalm 1, seems to walk in the way of scoffers? Who can trust a God who for so long appears apathetic to evil and injustice and who, when He finally rouses Himself to act, uses the Babylonians to do the job? That's like using a butcher with a cleaver for a task that calls for a surgeon with a scalpel. It's like firebombing an entire village to try to smoke out a single culprit. It's like wielding a sledgehammer where a jeweler's tool is needed.

It's like using Bin Laden to bring America to its knees.

How could God allow such a thing?

Habakkuk throws that challenge skyward, then stands on the watchtower and waits.

He doesn't have to wait long.

But some people do. Some people's lives get stalled here. They hurl their question skyward and watch to see what God will answer. They wait. They spend long nights and gray mornings waiting, scanning the unbroken sky for a sign. Any sign. Dramatic, subtle, gigantic, minuscule—anything at all that signals divine response. And they get nothing. Still they wait. After many seasons, they give up.

Ruth A. Tucker writes:

Where is God in the vastness of the universe? Where is God among the billions of stars and billions of light years and billions of people on this planet? Easy answers ring hollow. The unruffled, childlike faith of bygone years seems insufficient in the face of scientific discoveries that all too easily engulf God in a black hole. When I look into the night sky, I sometimes wonder whether my faith is a figment of my imagination. Where is God—not the God of the Big Bang, not the unmoved mover, not the ground of our being, but God—this very personal God of the Bible who knows me and who knows my every thought?[3]

Where is God when He won't answer me, or when His answers defy all my most cherished convictions about Him?

God's second answer to Habakkuk, though it comes swiftly enough, is almost as frustrating and cryptic as His first. Basically, God says, "Wait a little longer. Trust Me. The evil of the Babylonians will double back on them in time. Their very destructiveness carries the seeds of their own destruction."[4]

In some ways, this again seems like no answer at all.

Habakkuk's debate with God distills the problem of evil. Theologians have a name for this problem: theodicy. Theodicy is our attempt to defend God's goodness and sovereignty in the face of evil—monumental evil, predatory evil, institutional evil, personal evil, historical evil, demonic evil. Its key question is, *How can a loving and all-powerful God allow such evil to exist, let alone flourish?* Why Hitler, Stalin, Charles Manson, Idi Amin, Osama bin Laden? Why apartheid, genocide, homicide, suicide? Why so many villains living in palaces? Why so many saints living in hovels? Why leukemia? Why spina bifida and scoliosis and toxic spores and meningitis and metal fatigue in trains and electrical failure in planes and drunk drivers swerving across medians and scattering carloads of innocents?

Wait, God says. *Be patient. It will all work out in the end.* That answer is infuriating in its vagueness and insipidness. And if you doubt that, try spouting it to anyone who has just suffered devastating loss. The only people for whom this comes as a word of consolation are those who are not presently suffering. To the downtrodden, it is blather. To the heartbroken, it is near blasphemy. People *in extremis* are not much concerned about what works out in the end. They are wrung out in the agony of the *now.*

I have stood alongside people numb or raw with grief. People whose pain verges on madness. This is one of a pastor's dark honors. A few times, I have been the bearer of terrible news: the one to tell a young father that his wife has been in an accident and that his four-year-old daughter was flung forty feet from the vehicle, that she is comatose and critically injured and may not make it; the one to walk with a mother and father into the dim coolness of a morgue and hold them up as the coroner pulls pack the white sheet to reveal their teenage son lying very still beneath; the one to meet with a woman whose family has just been wiped out in a gruesome murder-suicide, as she howls with anguish, screaming over and over, "Why, why, why?"; the one to knock on the door of a woman whose husband, driving home one bright fall afternoon, probably whistling as he usually did, was killed instantly when an old man coming the other way had a stroke behind the wheel and veered into him, and she is trying to explain to her children why Daddy isn't coming home tonight or tomorrow night or the night after that.

The last word people need to hear at such moments is that God, at some distant point in the future, in some intangible, mystical way, works all things together for *good*.

IN THE MIDDLE OF GOD'S second response to Habakkuk, He says something that is the key to the whole book. It's the key to the whole question of whether God is good. It's the key, in fact, to the whole of life.

"The righteous," He says, "will live by his faith."[5]

At first blush, this seems cold comfort yet again. An ice

pack applied to a ruptured organ. A tin shack erected against a typhoon.

But it's infinitely more than that. It is, in fact, a truth utterly basic to life. The core of the Christian life is to live by faith.

And faith is finally this: resting so utterly in the character of God—in the ultimate goodness of God—that you trust Him even when He seems untrustworthy.

>- >- >-

I SAW FAITH LIKE THAT last March. It was Sunday afternoon, the first springlike day we had seen that year. Daffodils with petals like tilted teacups and hyacinth with flowers like miniature grape clusters lined our pathway. Our cherry trees were covered in a thick froth of blossoms. The scent in the air was both sweet and pungent. I had just awoken, mellow and floppy-limbed, from my ritual post-sermon nap. Some good friends had come over, and we were standing outside in the backyard, deciding what we were going to make for dinner. We'd decided it would be chicken.

The phone rang. We ran inside and went through the usual scramble under sofa pillows and scattered newspapers to find the thing. After five or six rings, my wife, Cheryl, found the phone and picked it up.

"No," she said. "No, no, no." Her voice was like the voice King David must have cried out in when the messenger told him his son Absalom was never coming home again: "O my son Absalom! O Absalom, my son, my son!"[6] Our friends and children had come in by now. We stood, helpless, watching Cheryl's face twist with every word. Whatever the news was, it struck her like cold nails driven through warm flesh. She was pale and trembling.

She put down the phone. We waited for her to speak. It took her several moments. Then...

"It's Big Dave," she said. "Big Dave is dead."

Big Dave. Dave, at eighteen, looked like a cross between Genghis Khan and the Buddha. One person described him this way: "He's as big as Goliath, but has the heart of King David." He was magnificently large, over three hundred pounds on a six-foot frame. He already had enough facial hair to sport a biker goatee: a thin, tapering, cloven thing, like the imprint of an impala's hoof around his mouth. He looked menacing, a monolith of brawn and girth. I once tried to move him from a spot. I heaved and leapt against him, ran headlong at him, battering-rammed his belly. He just stood, silent and stolid and unmoving, and then he clamped my shoulders in his massive hands and picked me up like I was a gunnysack of squirming field mice.

But he was gentle and deeply kind. He loved children, and they loved him. Often, I'd see him from a distance, four or five children hanging off him, a couple more tucked under his tree-trunk arms. He had a sly smile, and I'd hail him, and his mouth would crimp, and he'd nod ever so slightly. Carol, our youth pastor, has a photo of him in her office. He is dressed in a Friar Tuck costume, and his hair is bleached blond on top with inky black roots underneath, so that it looks like a chocolate cake with white frosting.

I baptized David in a lake the spring before. It took two of us to get him down and back up again. We plunged him hard and deep beneath the cold surface, and as we pulled him up the water fell off him in cataracts, rushing down his arms and chest and face. He stood up straight and embraced me in his huge arms, and I knew I was helpless, that he could crush me with those arms, pulverize me to a sodden mass, break me to splinters. But I knew, as well, that he'd never do it. With those arms, he'd only ever lift, receive, impart, protect, embrace.

I knew that the day Big Dave came with his parents to meet me about joining the church. I interviewed his parents, John and Justine, and that went well. Then I turned to David. "What about you?" I asked. "Where are you at?"

When David and his family showed up at our church, he was angry, sullen, stung raw with insult. He'd lived most of his life on the brunt side of rejection. People feared him and mocked him because of his size. Few had stopped long enough to know him. He had gone to several schools and several youth groups, and everywhere it was the same story: shunning, derision, slurs, taunts.

But our youth pastor, Carol, has never tolerated such

things among our youth. She has made cliquishness and gossip the oddity, the embarrassment, the thing you wouldn't be caught dead doing. And so Big-D, for the first time in his life, experienced love from his peers. He belonged. In fact, he more than belonged: Big-D was a hero to our youth, to our children, and increasingly, to our adults. I recognized leadership ability in him, and almost weekly I'd walk up beside Dave and say the same thing: "David, you're a leader. Leaders lead, and people follow. But you have to decide whether you're going to lead them up, or lead them down. David, lead up." I said that probably forty times to Big-D. I said it so often that, when he saw me coming, he'd simply repeat it to me: "I'm a leader. Leaders lead. I'm going to lead people up."

"What about you? Where are you at?" I asked that day in my office.

Big-D was tongue-tied. I asked him if he was ready to be baptized, and he said he thought so. He wasn't sure. We talked about baptism, what it means—a holy pantomime of dying and rising with Jesus, of new birth through the Spirit, of cleansing through Christ's blood. "David," I asked, "Do you belong to Christ?"

"I'm not sure."

"Do you want to belong to Christ?"

"Yes."

"Do you want to be sure that you belong to Christ?"

"Yes."

So I led David, and he spoke a prayer of surrender and invitation to Jesus, simple and heartfelt. He wept and laughed. We all did. And then we stood, and we hugged, and I knew then that this boy, this man, had the strength to rend me to pieces but not the heart for it. The gentleness of the Good Shepherd was in him.

"Big-D is dead."

And God is good?

He had been with some of the youth on an afternoon trip to a local island. They had walked the stony beach and were getting ready to climb into the boat and come home. But Big-D wanted to see the view from atop the cliff above the shore. It was maybe ninety feet up. He climbed the steep, slippery path along the edge of the embankment, grabbing tree trunks, tree roots, well-lodged stones, and bramble to pull himself up. He was tired, breathing heavy, drenched in sweat. Near the top, a large boulder, embedded in the ground, perched at the edge of the cliff. What David didn't notice is that the boulder sat on a ledge of soft earth that was deeply eroded, that curled underneath like a cresting wave, that hung suspended in midair, that was cantilevered over empty space and held together by only rock and water and a thin web of tree roots.

David sat on the boulder.

And everything gave way—earth, stone, root, man. David fell without a sound, falling through the air with a strange grace. No angel to catch him. He hit the ground with a terrible thud. The youth who were with him ran over. One young man, Nathan, was a paramedic, and he administered, hopelessly, mouth-to-mouth, CPR, the whole routine. Over and over and over, begging David to wake up, praying as he worked, until finally the medics showed up and told him to stop.

Big-D was dead.

Carol and I met half an hour later in the parking lot of the townhouse complex where David's parents lived. We were the ones to break the news. We looked at each other, too raw to speak. We prayed. But honestly, I hardly believed in God right then. I was angry with Him, if He was there at all. This was the third sudden, tragic death of a young man to hit our church in under three months. Driving to meet Carol, I had a blistering argument with God, and I did all the talking: "That's it. I will do this, and then I'm gone. You can find some other errand boy to run about, placating people, whistling in the dark, telling everyone You're good, You're running the show, everything's working out fine. That's bunk. This is my final gig."

Carol and I walked to the house and knocked on the door. Dave's mom, Justine, opened the door and she lit up. What good fortune, two pastors come for a visit on a Sunday afternoon!

"Look who's here to see us," she called to John, and he came over to the door, grinning. But they could tell, looking at the two of us, something was wrong, terribly wrong, and they stopped smiling.

"We have some very bad news," Carol said. "I think you need to sit down."

"What?" Justine said. "Tell us. What?"

"I think you should sit down."

"No. Tell us. What?"

"There's been an accident. David's dead."

And then I saw a miracle.

Justine began to worship. The first words out of her mouth were, "O God, You chose him, You chose my David. O Lord, thank You that You chose him, and he is with You right now, seeing You face-to-face. He's dancing in Your throne room right now. Lord, I love him. I love You. I miss my son, Lord. I need Your strength. But thank You that You chose him."

I repented. We all wept. And, strange and beautiful as it was, we all worshiped.

The full brunt of David's death hit Justine later, but not once did she stop taking her grief to God, turning it into worship, shaping it into prayer. I've watched her this past month, as our church finished a building project. Every day, she came to the church and painted murals on the walls of the children's wing—big, bright pictures of dancing children and fluttering blue jays and grazing giraffes and watchful angels, and a huge sun perched over all of it, smiling down.

Big-D loved children.

As I've watched her, I've realized that she knows God in a

way I want to know Him. Justine is not inclined to pore over books of theology, to delve into doctrinal subtleties. She does something more: She trusts God and rests in His character, His goodness, even when she can't explain Him.

The hardest thing for her has been letting go of the dreams she had for her son. She wanted to be there when he fell in love, when he came home to announce he was engaged, when he stood at the head of the church and watched his bride walk down the aisle. She wanted to see what God was going to do with his gift of leadership and his love for children. One day, a few months after the funeral, Justine got up in church and, in a thin, teary voice, read a poem she wrote. As she went, her voice grew stronger, bolder, declarative. The poem is called "A Mother's Dreams Are in the Father's Hands":

You called David home,
And I must let go
Of the dreams I had for him.
I know he is in my Father's hands.

I had dreams for David,
That he would finish school
And for a job he would enjoy,
Because whatever he set his heart to,
He knew You would help him through.

Yes, Lord, today I place these dreams
I had for David
In my Father's hands,
Knowing You will help me let go.

I had dreams for David,
His first love, where it was returned to him
By the one that would become his wife,
The one that would be the mother of his children,
The grandchildren they would share with me.
They would teach the children about God,
And they would grow to love Jesus.

Yes, Lord, today I place these dreams
I had for David
In my Father's hands,
Knowing You will help me let go.

I had dreams for David,
That he would grow to be a man,
That he would grow to love You, Lord,
And make my God his own
And share the love You had for him with others.

I had dreams for David,
That one day he would see You face-to-face.
Thank You, Father God,
For making this dream come true in You.

This is one dream I can hold onto,
Spending eternity with You.[7]

I've learned from Justine one of my best and deepest lessons yet as a pastor, as a Christian, as a man: the need to know God so well that, even though He slay me, yet will I worship Him. Because He's good.

Chapter Three

THE TESTIMONY
OF LEAVES

God's Faithfulness

Aleaf. Behold a single leaf. So fragile, it tears like paper, crushes in your hand to a moist stain, sharply fragrant. Dry, it burns swift and crackling as newsprint, pungent as gunpowder. Yet a leaf may withstand hurricanes, stubbornly clinging to its limb.

Hold it open in your palm. It is perfect as a newborn's smile. Pinch its stem between thumb and forefinger and hold it to the light. Eden bleeds through. Its veins are like bone work in silhouette. This single leaf, joined to the tree, drinks poison from the air, drinks it serenely as Socrates downing his cup of hemlock, and refuses to return in kind, instead spilling out life-giving oxygen. This leaf tilts to catch the sun, its warmth and radiance, to distill the heat and light down to the shadows, down to the roots, back up to limbs. To shade the earth. To feed you and me.

A leaf. God makes these season after season, one after the other, billions upon billions, from the Garden to the New Jerusalem, most for no eye but His own. He does it faithfully, or else I would not live to tell about it, or you to hear.

Perhaps of all my many sins against heaven, this ranks with the worst: Until this moment, I have never thanked God for a single leaf.

Which is the problem with faithfulness: We hardly notice it. Faithfulness is, by definition, the predictable, the habitual, the sturdy, the routine. It is the evidence of *things seen*, but seen so often we've grown blind to them. It is the substance of things expected, expected so unthinkingly that we now take them for granted.

It is the air we breathe, the ground we walk on, the skin we inhabit, the way our insides tick and pulse and spin all on their own, in season and out, whether we sleep or work or play, without asking us or us having to ask. It is these myriad amazing things—toes and eyes, leaf veins and cloudbursts, bedrock and ozone, seed and sap—that by their very constancy and durability have worn familiar or become invisible. The sheer steadfastness of things that surround and uphold us are dull with the caking of the ordinary. We live amidst surpassing wonders, but most of it has become run-of-the-mill. We dwell among endless miracles that, repeated day after day, have grown tedious. We are lavished with gifts that we now expect or ignore or begrudge.

Faithfulness bores us.

Who among us leapt up this morning as the sun rose, exclaiming, "Look! Look, everybody, look! The sun! Here it comes! Hallelujah, it's here again!"? Or who ran through the house shouting, "Ha ha—air! Behold! Air! Clean air, fresh air, air to fill my lungs, air to shape my words, air to move the clouds, air to lift the birds"?

Not me. I woke up groaning.

Philip Yancey writes:

> I remember my first visit to Old Faithful in Yellowstone National Park. Rings of Japanese and German tourists surrounded the geyser, their video cameras trained like weapons on the famous hole in the ground. A large digital clock stood beside the spot, predicting twenty-four minutes before the next eruption.
>
> My wife and I passed the countdown in the dining room of Old Faithful Inn overlooking the geyser. When the digital clock reached one minute, we, along with every other diner, left our seats and rushed to the windows to see the big, wet event.
>
> I noticed immediately, as if on signal, a crew of busboys and waiters descended on the tables to refill water glasses and clear

away dirty dishes. When the geyser went off, we tourists oohed and aahed and clicked our cameras; a few spontaneously applauded. But, glancing back over my shoulder, I saw that not a single waiter or busboy—not even those who had finished their chores—looked out the huge windows. Old Faithful, grown entirely too familiar, had lost its power to impress them.[1]

In both creation and relationships, faithfulness is the most amazing yet least captivating trait. It is one quality—in the cosmos, in God, in others—that we can't live without, but that we don't much live *with,* either, mindful of it, thankful for it.

Look how we use the word itself in everyday speech. "My husband. How can I describe him? Let me say this: He's faithful." Code language for *he's a drudge, a bean counter, a plodder. He gets the job done, but with no aplomb or pizzazz.* If we call a car faithful, we mean it's functional, not fast, not flashy. It's drab and boxy, an old dray horse.

Faithfulness is not only boring. In some contexts, it's almost embarrassing.

J. Allan Petersen, in *The Myth of the Greener Grass,* tells the story of a dozen married women at lunch together. The conversation got more and more intimate, under the skin, the sharp tip of inquiry corkscrewing into inmost places, prying loose tightly held secrets. "How many of you," one woman asked, "have been faithful to your husbands?"

Only one woman out of the twelve raised her hand.

At home that evening, one of the women who *didn't* raise her hand told her husband about the lunch, the question, her reaction. "But," she quickly added, "I *have* been faithful."

"Then why didn't you raise your hand?"

"I was ashamed."[2]

GOD'S FAITHFULNESS IS one divine characteristic that we rest in so completely that our rest has become apathy. "In him," Paul declares, "we live and move and have our being."[3] We just hustle in, heads down, duty-bound, and clear the table.

So our dilemma: How do we rest in God's faithfulness, but never take it for granted?

Maybe the best way to begin is to examine how God describes His own faithfulness. Allow me to summarize the biblical texts on this theme.

He abounds in faithfulness, and by faithfulness He keeps His covenant of love to a thousand generations. Because of His faithfulness, He does no wrong. He shows Himself faithful to the faithful. He's faithful in all He does, and by it He guarantees that His words are right and true. His faithfulness reaches to the skies, is sent down from the heavens, and is appointed to protect us like a shield and a rampart. God's faithfulness surrounds Him and goes out before Him. He will not betray it, and it endures forever.

In faithfulness, God disciplines His children. Because of His faithfulness, He will keep all His promises. His faithfulness is great. It is not canceled out by our lack of faith. Because of it, He forgives us and cleanses us from confessed sin, and He will not allow us to be tempted beyond what we can bear. By His faithfulness, God sanctifies us and keeps us blameless until the coming of Jesus, and by it He gives us strength and protection from the evil one. Faithfulness is one of Jesus' names. What's more, the faithfulness of God is connected with His love, righteousness, truthfulness, steadfastness, compassion, mercy, peace, grace, slowness to anger, creative power, mightiness, justice, deliverance, relief, and holiness.[4]

Old Faithful indeed.

There's a common thread in all this: you and me. The touchstone of God's faithfulness is His way with people. It is mostly about a journey He took, His house to yours, in order to bring you all the way back again to His. Behind the drama of the incarnation, the atonement, the redemption; behind the drama of Jesus calling Zacchaeus down from the sycamore tree, calling Peter away from his nets, calling Matthew away from the tax booth, calling you from wherever you were when He found you; behind all that is simply this: God is true to Himself. God is faithful.

His faithfulness began far back, first in creation, then through various covenants. Four thousand years ago, God made covenant with Abraham. Through Abraham, He chose a people for Himself, a people to walk in His ways, live by His grace, trust in His Word, display His character. He *promised* all this.

But here's the rub: He guaranteed the promise by *His* own faithfulness, not Abraham's. Abraham, left to his own, driven by his own anxiety and shortsightedness, would keep passing his wife off as his sister, would keep siring Ishmaels. Abraham, like other people I know, was fickle. He was too skittish, too slipshod of will and wayward of heart to uphold the magnitude of the promise. A promise this big—this cosmic, this historic, this intimate—needed to be established on something more solid than human willingness or ability.

It needed God's faithfulness.

The story is told in Genesis 15. God promises Abraham He will make him a mighty nation, and through him and his seed to bless all nations. To establish the promise, God *cuts covenant* with Abraham. This was an ancient ritual, in which the covenant partners hewed an animal in two. The severed pieces were laid out facing each other, a pathway marked between them. The partners of the covenant walked this pathway, between the bloody halves of the carcass. This was to enact two things: a pledge to walk within the bounds of their promise, and a willingness, if they didn't, to suffer the same fate as that animal, to be hewn and scattered.

Always, both partners walked the pathway.

Except in this instance. Here, all the other elements of cutting covenant are in place—the promise, the halved animal, the two pieces laid out, a pathway between. Only this time, just one covenant partner walks the pathway. God alone does.[5]

The covenant, the vastness of its promise, depends on God alone.

Later, the writer of Hebrews comments on this:

> When God made his [covenant with] Abraham, since there was no one greater for him to swear by, he swore by himself.... Because God wanted to make the unchanging nature of his purpose very clear to the heirs of what was promised, he confirmed it with an oath. God did this so that, by two unchangeable things [the promise and the oath] in which it is impossible for God to lie, we who have fled to take hold of the hope offered to us may be greatly encouraged. We have this hope as an anchor for the soul, firm and secure.[6]

God is faithful. *An anchor for the soul, firm and secure.*

God is true to Himself. *By the promise and the oath, two unchangeable things in which it is impossible for God to lie.*

We may be greatly encouraged.

We can rest in this.

TRUE TO HIMSELF. We've grown infatuated with that phrase. We rarely use it anymore, though, to describe God. We use it instead as a superlative of human decisiveness, integrity, sincerity: *That man is true to himself.*

To be true to yourself is our highest creed, our one orthodoxy, our most deeply cherished ethical tenet. It's our Magna Carta. *Be true to yourself.* No further justification or explanation is needed. It carries its own inherent authority.

But there's one tiny problem. Most despots are true to themselves. Most predators, swindlers, and sexual deviants are true to themselves. And forget casting the baleful eye at *those* people. Look at you. Look at me. In any one of us, there are these huge untamed tracts of rudeness and cowardice, big uncultivated swaths of deviousness and waywardness. Me? I'm a jostling, bulging gunnysack of bad thoughts and nasty impulses, the whole load howling to be let out.

Who decides what my true self is that I should be true to it? What touchstone do I use? I've found that, to live in Truth, I have to jettison at least half my own strongest wishes. I have to spend at least as much time denying myself as being true to myself.[7]

But here's the good news: God is different. God is true to Himself, and the self God is true to is true. I might write a book one day on divine limitations, the things God *cannot* do: lie, sin, remember confessed sin, break a promise, cease to be God. *Unchangeable things in which it is impossible for God to lie.* These are God's holy handicaps. His own nature prohibits them.

He must be true to Himself, and His very essence is truth.

BUT IS THAT TRUE? God disappoints us, at a personal level, at a cosmic level, at a theological level. God at times seems distracted, indifferent, capricious. As a pastor, I have sat with many people clinging to one of God's promises like shipwrecked sailors clutching pieces of shattered hull: *He'll sanctify my spouse. His word will not return void. He will do more than I ask or imagine. He will work all things together for good.*

But their grip is slipping, and God seems to have gone away on a very long trip and forgotten to send a postcard.

But I have also seen this: Here, especially here—in this silence, this darkness, this loneliness, this sorrow—many people meet the God of the brokenhearted. This is the God who sometimes just sits with us, silent, shadowy. This, too, is part of the Holy Wild where we meet the God whom Elijah knew, not in the exhilaration of the mountaintop, but in the loneliness of the cave, in the smallness of a whisper after windstorm and firestorm. The God whose faithfulness is displayed, sometimes in storm and fire, but more often in bread enough for today, arriving in the most surprising ways.[8]

There are terrible times when God breaks in and sends to us, as with Elijah, ravens with food in their beaks. Times when He lifts us, as with Jeremiah, up with rags from the well we've been thrown into, or lowers us, as with Paul, down in a basket along the city wall to rescue us from our enemies. And there are other terrible times when God doesn't show up in any of those ways, but shows us something of Himself anyhow. Both times are an expression of His faithfulness.

The apostle Paul celebrated loud and long and eloquently the unfailing faithfulness of God. Yet what was his experience? "We were under great pressure, far beyond our ability to endure, so that we despaired even of life. Indeed, in our hearts we felt the sentence of death."[9]

Later, he gets down to stark, sordid details:

> [I've] been in prison...been flogged...exposed to death again and again. Five times I received...the forty lashes minus one. Three times I was beaten with rods, once I was stoned, three times I was shipwrecked. I spent a night and a day in the open sea, I have been constantly on the move. I have been in danger from rivers, in danger from bandits, in danger from my own

countrymen, in danger from Gentiles; in danger in the city, in danger in the country, in danger at sea; and in danger from false brothers. I have labored and toiled and have often gone without sleep; I have known hunger and thirst and have often gone without food; I have been cold and naked. Besides everything else, I face daily the pressure of my concern for all the churches.[10]

And yet Paul could, in the same letter and without any sense of contradiction, write:

But this happened that we might not rely on ourselves but on God, who raises the dead. He has delivered us from such a deadly peril, and he will deliver us. On him we have set our hope.[11]

Is Paul looking in the face of monumental suffering and whistling a happy tune? Is he suffering from willful blindness? Frivolous optimism? Rigid dogmatism? I have a Jewish friend who insists that to speak of God as virtuous—good, wise, loving, faithful—after the tragedy and the travesty of the Holocaust is to blaspheme.

But Paul tasted his own holocaust. And he didn't for a minute think that suffering—his own or that of others—canceled out God's faithfulness. In fact, his point in mentioning his own sufferings is to set them against the backdrop of God's faithfulness. His catalog of being wounded and hounded climaxes with the declaration that Christ's grace is *sufficient*. Paul was driven, Job-like, to the end of himself where he discovered, Job-like, the God who would never leave or forsake him. [12]

In a likewise remarkable passage, Hebrews lists the varied sufferings of the heroes of the faith—"some faced jeers and flogging, while still others were chained and put in prison. They were stoned; they were sawed in two; they were put to death by the sword. They went about in sheepskins and goatskins, destitute, persecuted and mistreated…they wandered in deserts and mountains, and in caves and holes in the ground"—all that to conclude this: *We should not lose heart* but instead press on, fixing our eyes on Jesus, the author and perfecter of our faith. [13]

False things must shatter before real things shine through.

John and Linda Polus come to mind. They showed up one January. They had traveled in their sailboat from Oregon, along the alternately wild and serene coastline, taking their time, pushed by tailwinds or tacking against crosswinds and headwinds, motoring along when all winds failed, slow and steady until they came to Canada. There, they decided to winter in a harbor just ten minutes from our church.

Few people smile as much as John and Linda or with such deep-down radiance. Their faces have that red, shiny brightness that people get when they've fallen asleep too close to an open fire. And they live with their arms wide open, figuratively and often literally, a gesture of both relinquishment and receiving. They're both musical and got involved with that part of our church. Linda played the piano and sang. John sang also and played the guitar, helped with the sound, and ran photocopies. We fell in love with them, and they with us.

One Palm Sunday, we had a film crew in our church service, shooting footage that we later edited into a video. We had baptisms that day, and my favorite part of the video is during the baptisms. The cameraman caught John's face, watching, listening. I don't think John knew the camera's eye was on him—he looks so childlike, so guileless. He's got that radiance, that burnished skin, that instinctive gesture of blessing. He's got that laughing smile, like someone's tickling him, lightly, playfully. His is a look of utter contentment, pure wonder, wanting nothing and thankful for everything. A cat in a patch of sunlight. He's rapturous, in all the ways you can imagine that.

What you'd never guess is that he was once an angry man, his anger like an Arctic storm, wild and implacable, until the Lion of Judah subdued and revived him. What you'd never guess is that Linda has cancer, and that this very week she's been having other symptoms—dizziness, blurred vision, numbness in her hands—and that by week's end she'll be diagnosed with multiple sclerosis. By Easter Sunday they will have moved away, and she will sometimes be staggering and sightless with the stalking symptoms of her diseases; her movements stiff and choppy; her seeing thickly shrouded; her hair falling out in great sheaves on her pillow, in fistfuls in the shower, in massive skeins in her brush; and her skin will be red and shiny from something besides inner joy—from radiation scorching her insides like a branding iron.

But they keep trusting in God's faithfulness.

Count it all joy, my brothers, when you go through trials of many kinds. So says James.[14] I've sometimes wondered if he knew what he was talking about. Had he been a pastor long enough, lived among the broken and the sorrowing long enough, to have any idea? But, of course, he knows. And John and Linda somehow got his counsel so deep-set in their bones that nothing now can drive it out. For them, everything is an occasion for thanksgiving. For them, everything is evidence of God's faithfulness.

They have visited a few times since that Easter when they went away. We eat with them. We pray with them. We ask God to heal Linda. And we ask Him for strength, for them and for us, but mostly for us, because we feel weak. We are lovesick and heartsick whenever they come near.

God always answers our prayers for strength, and almost always He does it through John and Linda themselves. If we've doubted in some way that God is good, God is in control, God is filled with mercy and grace—that God is *faithful*—John and Linda remind us that it's so. They do this *without even trying.*

They just stand there with enormous smiles on their bright, upturned faces, mirthful as Bacchus, arms stretched winglike beneath our prayers, drenching in them like farmers in the rain that ends a long drought.

John sent this e-mail recently:

> I got your e-mail the other day and I've been thinking so much about faith ever since. Other people have commented about our trust and faith in GOD, yet we feel that His faithfulness to us is what is getting us through. He has shined so bright through all of this that it would take a tremendous effort not to trust Him. HE is doing it all—not us! Your e-mail encouraged me to reexamine and rethink Hebrews 11 (always one of my favorite chapters). I've always been in such awe of people with that kind of faith, and the writer does tell us they should be commended. But I have a new perspective now. How awesome God is to show Himself to us so clearly that we can have faith, trust, and comfort in barren and tragic circumstances. I also took another look at Ephesians 2:8; I always thought that "this not from yourselves, it is the gift of God" referred to grace. But now, I think maybe it's referring

to the faith mentioned. Maybe this is "old hat" to everyone, but it's a real shift in thinking for me. It makes me more in awe of God than ever before, and shows me just how little I really am. I hope this makes sense.

Love,

John[15]

I hope this makes sense. Yes, John, perfect sense. For you know the God who is true to Himself.

༒ ༒ ༒

WHEN THE SEAS ROAR and the mountains give way, we despair, or we take hold of God. His faithfulness is made known in countless things—sun and rain, food and air, shelter and freedom, health and safety. But God never guarantees those things. They are expressions of His faithfulness, but not its essence.

There are actually only three things God promises with a guarantee. In these three things, God is always true to Himself. These three things are the bedrock of His faithfulness. They are the utterly trustworthy things that God promises on the basis of His own character. *We have this hope as an anchor for the soul, firm and secure.* These three things are the aspects of God's faithfulness in which, no matter what else goes amiss, we can rest completely.

Three things.

God is faithful to forgive our sins if we confess them: "If we confess our sins, he is faithful and just and will forgive us our sins and purify us from all unrighteousness."[16] He is true to Himself in that.

God is faithful to make us holy and blameless before Christ: "May God himself, the God of peace, sanctify you through and through. May your whole spirit, soul and body be kept blameless at the coming of our Lord Jesus Christ. The one who calls you is faithful and *he will do it.*"[17] No one who trusts in Him will be found wanting on the day of judgment. He is true to Himself in that.

And God is faithful to get us home.

There was a moment early in the ministry of Jesus' disciples when they experienced amazing success. They cast out demons, healed the sick, preached the good news. They returned, giddy and heady with triumph, and told Jesus all they had done.

Jesus was excited for them, filled with joy on their behalf.

"*However,*" he told them, "do not rejoice that the spirits submit to you, *but rejoice that your names are written in heaven.*"[18]

Do not rejoice in the circumstantial, the insubstantial, the ephemeral. Do not rejoice in what can be here today, gone tomorrow, in things whose roots are in thin soil, whose footings are in sand. Do not rejoice in what depends on you. Do not rejoice in what God may bless you with but never guarantees.

Rejoice that your name is written in heaven. It's written there, not by your hand or by your work, but by God alone. God alone made a way for you to live with Him forever. God alone walked between the halves of the bloody carcass. God alone became the bloody carcass.

None of it depends on you.

It all depends on the God who promised.

And He is always true to Himself.

I SAW QUEEN ELIZABETH II ONCE, when I was a boy of twelve. She visited our northern city on a cold day in spring. I was enlisted, with a number of school bands, to play my snare drum—a crisp, snapping series of rolls—as part of the city's welcoming ceremony.

But she never got out of the car. She was running late and so had to forgo all our well-rehearsed public sentiments and ceremonies. Instead, her limousine took a slow pass, a single lap, around the track field at our city park. The crowd pressed in to see. I had to stand where I was and saw only people's backs. But just as her coach passed in front of where I stood, the crowd parted—miraculous as the Red Sea—and a thin sliver of view cracked open, like a camera shutter momentarily sticking.

I saw her. Her stolid face. Her blank eyes. Her one hand raised, rigid as a prosthetic arm. Her white glove in the car window like a fish back flashing up from murky depths, almost in a gesture of dismissal or warning.

It was, I suppose, a kind of faithfulness—showing up, city after city, to hold up that stiff gloved hand for children who cradle armloads of flowers they will never be able to give you; for fathers holding infants aloft to behold, over the heads of the onlookers, a sight that to the child means nothing; to hear (or not) school bands play their squawky renditions of *O Canada;* to hear (or not) mayors make nervous, stilted speeches.

It was a kind of faithfulness.

But God comes into our midst afoot, with a mighty and outstretched arm, making intimate friends as He goes; talking to anyone who wishes; delightedly receiving from us the flowers He Himself crafted; inviting us, if we're willing, to come home with Him and stay. And even, when no one's noticing, one by one, making leaves.

That's faithfulness.

Chapter Four

A VISITOR
IN THE CAMP

God's Love

S ally Field, with heartbreaking candor, played a Depression-era widow fighting to save her cotton farm in the 1984 movie *Places in the Heart*. She won the Oscar for it. Academy Awards speeches are usually just a string of dithering tributes, a gust of giddiness and flattery. Occasionally, some prophet manqué will use the platform to deliver a caustic political diatribe, chastising the very people who have made him rich and renowned.

But not Sally Field. Sally wasn't giddy, or flattering, or caustic, or angry. What she was—starkly, startlingly, shamelessly—was needy. She clutched the Oscar tight, like a scared waif holding a rag doll, and blurted, "I can't deny the fact you like me—right now, you like me."

The sad thing was, she was wrong. *They* didn't really like her, and in the days and weeks that followed, Sally was mocked heartlessly for her vulnerability. I think of her from time to time and wonder if she still craves approval, acceptance, *if she still needs to know they like her.* In 1984, she was at the height of her accomplishments, her beauty, her influence. She had wealth, fame, power.

But beneath it all she was a little girl looking for love.

Back in my first church, I used to get an occasional phone call from a man named Sonny. He always called on Sunday afternoon, which is a pastor's hibernating season. Sonny would contact a general operator and have him or her track down a pastor, any pastor, whichever pastor was available. I'm not sure how often he did this, but Sonny got ahold of me three, maybe four times in six years.

I'd accept the call, often groggy, and Sonny would come on at the other end. He was always weeping. It was as though the phone had dropped in a sea cavern, and all I could hear was emptiness punctuated by an occasional *drip, drip* from the cold walls. I would speak softly, tell Sonny to take his time. Then after a minute or two, he'd sputter out something, slurred and sodden, mostly incoherent. Eventually, I'd quiet him, console him as best I could, pray for him, and hang up.

But one time I feared he was going to kill himself. I insisted on coming to see him. He was cagey, then feisty, then resigned. He gave me his address, and I drove over.

Sonny said he was in his forties. He looked in his fifties. He lived in a single room in a shabby motel in the industrial part of town. The room stank of smoke, sweat, moldering things. Sonny did his best to keep things neat. But he, too, had a strong odor, the kind people get when their insides have started to rot. The kind of odor no amount of rinsing and dousing can hide. He jutted with bone. His clothes hung limp. He was jittery, like a man who spent his days dodging enemies, predators, shadows, ghosts. He couldn't sit still. Up, down, up, to and fro, his hands fluttering and twitching wildly in the air, as if he were swatting off a swarm of wasps. And then, suddenly, he'd slump, the air all run out of him, replaced with lead.

He told me he had nothing to live for.

"Sonny," I said, "Jesus loves you."

"Does He?" he asked, anguished, really wanting to know. Sonny had so many needs, so many problems, an army of social workers couldn't sort him out in a month of Sundays. But most of all, he wanted to know, *Am I loved?*

"Does He really?" he said. "I love Him so much. I wish I could know that He loved me. Do you think He loves me?"

And though I did, I wondered. For honestly, Sonny seemed the most unloved man on the earth.

Do you think He loves me?

Do you really like me?

If there's one thing that unites all of us—from Sally Field at the apex to Sonny in the pit—it's wanting to know that we're loved. *Do you think He loves me? Do you really like me?*

God so loved the world, John tells us.

But I can hear Sonny, his voice sharp with doubt, raw with grief: "Does He? Does He love *me?*"

MY FATHER USED TO MOCK my faith in a loving God. If there was a god at all, he said, he was bored and cruel, a trickster. On a whim he might starve a million babies. As a prank he might spark a genocidal war. With a flick of his finger, to amuse himself, he might kill and maim half a country with a mudslide, a flash flood, an earthquake, a typhoon. "As flies to wanton boys, are we to the gods," my father would say, quoting *King Lear*.[1]

"So much suffering and brutality and outright evil in the world," he'd say. "How can you believe in a loving God?"

Often I would retort with a shopworn argument, oiling up once more the old apologetic musket. "Where," I would ask him, "did you ever get the idea of *good* and *evil, right* and *wrong?* Did you think up those moral categories? How did you arrive at the position that killing and maiming and thievery are wrong? Not just a disruption to education and commerce, but downright *wrong?* If God is as you describe Him, then what lies outside yourself that you can make such judgments and expect them to have any validity, to be anything more than mere opinion? Don't you see, Dad, that your very yearning for the good, your capacity to know what it looks like, points to something Good beyond you—to a God who embodies the good?"

But he didn't. And, truthfully, the argument is logically airtight but emotionally sterile. It still leaves Sally pleading beneath the stage lights and Sonny weeping in his dismal room.

❧ ❧ ❧

THAT'S SOMETIMES WHAT we're left with: a piece of straw to splint a broken heart, a fistful of wishes to fill a lifetime of emptiness. Yet there's a funny irony in all this. It's often those with scant experience of God's love who rest in it best.

I'm thinking of history. I'm thinking of Jews and Christians. Jews and Christians who have at various times, in various places, suffered evil without pity. The Roman historian Tacitus wrote a line in *The Annals,* describing the emperor Nero's sadism toward Christians:

> Mockery of every kind was added to their deaths. Covered with the skins of beasts, they were torn by dogs and perished, or were nailed to crosses, or were doomed to the flames and burned, to serve as nightly illumination, when daylight had expired.
>
> Nero offered his gardens for the spectacle....[2]

The number of Christians martyred in the twentieth century far outstripped the combined number of martyrs in nineteen prior centuries, and in the infancy of this millennium there is no sign of the bloodshed abating. And the Jews, their suffering didn't begin in Germany in the 1930s and '40s. It was only consummated there. Persecution of the Jewish people began four thousand years ago and has carried on since, almost without interruption.

Yet strangely, it's these very ones—those who have suffered most deeply, generation after generation—who are often the first to testify to God's love. I think of my friend Helen, a Russian immigrant whose Baptist family perished in one of Stalin's concentration camps. She escaped into Germany, just a girl, and found herself conscripted into forced labor under Hitler. She came to Canada after the war and was raped by her cousin, the one person she trusted, the man who had promised her and the government that he would take care of her.

Helen's life has been a graveyard of loss, a scrap yard of betrayal. But ask her any day what she knows, and she'll tell you, "God is good. He loves me." Her conviction about that hasn't come by toting up her days of wounds and wars, weighing them against her days of laughter and bounty, and seeing which tips the scale. Her belief has a different taproot: God is simply who He says He is, regardless of what her troubles might have tempted her to think or surmise. Helen stands in a venerable tradition. She is part of that great cloud of witnesses who, living by faith, refuse to reduce God to their own experience, to limit His love by the evidence of their own circumstances.

Elie Wiesel tells the story of a group of Jewish men, ghoulishly withered, huddled together in a Nazi death camp. Yom Kippur, the Day of Atonement, comes. The oldest and frailest of them stands up. "Let us fast and pray for forgiveness, to atone for our many sins," he says.

One man is appalled at the idea. "We have to atone for our sins? What about God? Who allowed us to be in this misery? What about Him asking *our* forgiveness?"

There is silence, until finally the old man says, "And now, let us go and pray."[3]

That great cloud of witnesses who refuse to reduce God to their own experience.

God is love. That's what the apostle John declares.[4] And he goes further, and gets personal: "How great is the love the Father has lavished on us, that we should be called children of God! And that is what we are!"[5]

This is the Son of Thunder speaking, a man so hot-tempered, so rash, so bent on bully tactics, he wanted to call down fire from heaven to burn up an entire Samaritan village for being rude to him. This is the apostle who suffered exile and imprisonment for his faith, who himself spent time in a bleak prison camp. How did he know with such lucid, fervid certainty that God's essential nature is love—extravagant, sacrificial, heartbreaking, breathtaking love? How did he know with such cartwheeling joy that he was God's child, awash in love?

He was part of that great cloud of witnesses who refuse to reduce God to their own experience.

Left to our own, we come up with a portrait of God much like that of my father's: cruel, fickle, aloof, blundering. And yet, when we say it—God is love—something in the inmost part of us awakens and starts to sing. Deep calls to deep.

Here's how John puts it:

> This is how God showed his love among us: He sent his one and only Son into the world that we might live through him. This is love: not that we loved God, but that he loved us and sent his Son as an atoning sacrifice for our sins.[6]

This is the God who, though He allows us to taste misery along with joy, loves us so much that He comes into the camp alongside us. And not just to experience our misery but, it turns out, Himself to make atonement for us.

✺ ✺ ✺

I MENTIONED MY FLIMSY apologetics with my father, trying to convince him that his idea of justice, of cosmic right and wrong, was itself evidence of the Transcendent Lawgiver. I was right, but my rightness never moved my dad to repentance and faith. He never fell to his knees and, like doubting Thomas before the risen Christ, exclaimed, "My Lord and my God." Looking back now, I think I know why: I never invited him, as Jesus did with Thomas, to touch Jesus' wounds, to reach out his hand and put it where the nails drove through bone and muscle, where the spear pierced flesh and heart. My dad had a bitter childhood in many ways—a sick mother, a surly father, a feud with his brother—and the older I get, the more I think he struggled to reconcile *his experience* with the promise of God's love. It was hard for him to believe Christ was in the camp with him.

And so my argument, smacked down to trump him, never dealt with my Dad's real heart-cry, which is Sonny's, which is Sally Field's: Does *He love me?* Does He really?

Because no one is looking for transcendence in the midst of their doubt and grief. They're looking for the God who will stand with them in their little locked room, in their prison camp, bearing wounds, letting them touch Him.

I wonder if this very hunger we have to be loved is a sign of another kind: not of God's transcendence, but of His immanence, His being with us. I wonder if our lovesickness is in fact God's image, broken and gaunt but still potent, within us. It is the footfall or thumbprint of Another, evidence of Things Unseen, rumors of a Visitor in the camp. Tina Turner, the husky-voiced torch singer with the gyrating legs, used to belt out her refrain, "What's love got to do with it?" And then, more poignant, less defiant, almost pleading: "Who needs a heart when a heart can be broken?"

But why can hearts be broken? This dangerous vulnerability, this openness to another's joy and pain—could this be the divine image shimmering up in us? That we ourselves wound so easily—could this be a clue to the God who bears scars? The thinness of our heart's casing—could this hint at something of the spear-pierced heart of the Savior? *We love because He first loved us.* And maybe, too, we *need* love for the same reason: He first *loved* us and awoke love in us, and ever after we're haunted by our hunger for it. We have this instinct for love that won't quit, that is hardy and wily, irrational, spendthrift, naively stubborn. It keeps hitching its skirts and running to embrace knaves and prodigals.

Even after a lifetime of missing love, we still want it. But isn't this what God is like, seeking beauty in the ruins, pursuing love even when love seems quixotic, foolhardy, undignified, wasteful?

Karl Barth was asked once what was the most profound theological idea he'd ever thought or heard. This is a man who had waded through every bog of twenty centuries of theological reflection, swam in its every little inlet, poked down every narrow rabbit hole, mapped out every twisting maze. This is a man who wrote eight thick volumes of systematic theology and many other books besides. What was the most profound thing he'd ever thought or heard?

"Jesus loves me, this I know," he said, "for the Bible tells me so."

Those simple words can be the crown of a lifetime of insight, because this love came down, rose up, never stopped, and runs to embrace even you, even me.

The BBC made a television series back in the 1960s about Jesus called *The Son of Man*. Forget the angular, oracular, ethereal Jesus we've made a fetish of, the golden-haired *angelos* with the Shakespearean cadences in his speech. This Jesus is earthy, disheveled, potbellied, slovenly. He slurs and mumbles His words. He lurches about, drunken-sailor-like. It's shocking to watch today. But in the 1960s, in what was then still mostly a very prim, buttoned-down England, it was an outrage.

But some of the scenes come to life with huge, raw vitality. In one, Roman soldiers descend on a Jewish village, sacking, burning, beating. Women shriek. Men lie in pools of spilled blood. Jesus comes upon the destruction in its wake, after the soldiers have done their worst and left. People stand around, weeping, cursing, nursing wounds. Houses smolder in the background.

"You have heard it said," Jesus says, working the crowd like a rabble-rouser, "'Hate your enemy.' 'An eye for an eye, a tooth for a tooth!'"

The people howl, "Yes, yes! Gouge their eyes out. Break their teeth."

"Ah, yeah," Jesus says. Then He stops, looks around. "But *I* tell you, love your enemy."

"No!" they shout.

"Yes," Jesus says. "Love him, and if he strikes you on the cheek, give him the other to strike also."

They almost lynch Jesus.

But this is exactly how God loved us. While we were yet sinners, Christ died for us, the godly and the ungodly. *How great is the love the Father has lavished on us, that we should be called children of God. And that is what we are!* This is the love of God: an alchemy that can turn enemies into children.

CHRIST, RISEN YET WOUNDED, comes into the camp, comes into the locked room, runs down the road with His robes hitched up, to be with us.

Dennis Ngien, a Vietnamese Christian, tells this story:

> When I was eight years old, I lost my father to cancer. A week after his burial, I became severely ill.... I still remember how my mother, newly widowed, cared for me. She did not discuss with me how I felt. Instinctively she took me into her arms and caressed my back with her gentle hands, reassuring me with

84

words of comfort and love for me. I grew so sick that I was hospitalized. Since we lived in a remote village about ten miles from the hospital, my mother carried me there on her back, walking powerfully, uphill and down. With tears streaming down her cheek, she said: "Son, Daddy is not here. But Mommy is still here. Hang in there. We will make it to the hospital soon."

Ngien goes on:

This childhood experience confirmed for me that a love that does not suffer with the suffering of the beloved is not love at all. What consolation would it have been if my mother had remained aloof from my suffering?[7]

Love that does not suffer with the suffering of the beloved is not love at all.

Are you there, Sonny? Sally?

Listen. This is love: He enters the camp.

BUT HOW CAN WE REST IN THIS?

There's only one way, actually: to love as He loves. If Jesus shows the full extent of His love by washing feet, then we are "blessed" if we, too, do these things.[8]

"Dear friends," John writes, "since God so loved us, *we also ought to love one another*. No one has ever seen God; but if we love one another, God lives in us and his love is made complete in us."[9] And then this remarkable conclusion: "And so *we know and rely on the love God has for us*."[10]

God completes His love in us when we love one another. The only way we can get to the place where we rely on the love God has for us—where we rest in it—is by loving. He calls us, you and me, to be His kiss, His touch, His word, His embrace, and by doing so to also be assured of His kiss, touch, word, embrace. He calls me to Sonny's little room to be a living testimony of the Father's love. And, testifying to it, to be convinced afresh of it myself, for myself, for the world.

An excerpt from a letter written by a missionary couple in Brazil:

> Driving through the Christmas traffic, fighting the drizzling rain, I chanced on a four-year-old little girl. She was wet and cold and shaking. Her clothes were ragged, her hair

was matted, and her nose was running. She walked between the cars at the stoplight, washing headlights because she was too short to wash windshields. A few gave her coins, others honked at her to get away from their vehicles.

As I drove away only some fifty cents poorer, I raged at God for the injustice in the world that allowed the situation. "God, how could you stand by, helpless?" Later that evening, God came to me softly with that still small voice and responded not in like kind to my rage, but with tenderness, "I *have* done something. I created *you*."[11]

Since God so loved us, we also ought to love one another. No one has ever seen God; but if we love one another, God lives in us and His love is made complete in us. And so we know and rely on the love God has for us.

I am stumbling toward this. But I know enough to know this: Like God's forgiveness, God's love only becomes real to those who give it away. To rest here, we keep having to give our fifty cents' worth.

I had the privilege of studying under Gordon Fee, a leading New Testament scholar. When I studied with him, he had just completed a massive and authoritative commentary on 1 Corinthians. One day he was lecturing on this letter, and he came to chapter 13, the "love chapter." He read the first part of it.

> If I speak in the tongues of men and of angels, but have not love, I am only a resounding gong or a clanging cymbal. If I have the gift of prophecy and can fathom all mysteries and all knowledge, and if I have a faith that can move mountains, but have not love, I am nothing. If I give all I possess to the poor and surrender my body to the flames, but have not love, I gain nothing.
>
> Love is patient, love is kind. It does not envy, it does not boast, it is not proud. It is not rude, it is not self-seeking, it is not easily angered, it keeps no record of wrongs. Love does not delight in evil but rejoices with the truth. It always protects, always trusts, always hopes, always perseveres. Love never fails.[12]

Gordon Fee said that when he was writing his commentary and came to this passage, he sat a long time. He brooded, he fretted, he wondered what he could possibly add to it. What else was there to say? The most sublime piece of love poetry ever written. Why sully it with the slag of grammatical studies, the debris of speculative footnotes, the white noise of scholarly quibbles?

And then God spoke to him: "Gordon, do you understand, this is the way I love you?"

"Yes, Lord."

"Gordon, *what if it were not so?*"

And Gordon Fee, a big man, loud and brash, cried like a baby for an hour.

What if it were not so? What if God only loved as I did— proportionally, moderately, prudently, frugally, as it suited Him? When it was convenient. When there was charm in the other to woo Him. When there was something love-worthy in the other, something there to draw love out. When there was a twinge of guilt, a nagging sense of personal debt.

Fifty cents and that's all.

What if it were not so? What if God loved as I did?

But He didn't love that way. He loved us as only the God who *is* love can: with a washbasin, a wounded side, a fatted calf, a cross on His back, *while we were still enemies.* From inside the camp.

He loved us with all the riches of heaven, lavished on the least of these, the worst of sinners.

And the more we dare to love like Him, the more we will taste the reality of this love. We will start to rely on it. We'll put all our weight there.

My children have a book by Robert Munsch called *Love*

You Forever. A mother, from her youngest days with her child, through his terrible twos and his rebellious teens and into his distracted middle age, has a habit: She gathers her sleeping son in her arms, no matter how big he's grown, and cradles him to her side. And she sings over him, "I'll love you forever, I'll like you for always, as long as I'm living my baby you'll be."[13]

Which is how God loves you.

> "Do not fear.... Do not let your hands hang limp. The LORD your God is with you, he is mighty to save. He will take great delight in you, he will quiet you with his love, he will rejoice over you with singing."[14]

Sonny, are you there? Sally?
Yes, He loves you. He really loves you.

Part I I

STAND IN
THIS PLACE

*How God's Saving Nature
Is the Foundation of Our Salvation*

Chapter Five

A Burned Patch
of Ground

God's Wrath

New York journalist Charles Kuralt, a sophisticated big-city man, used to poke gentle fun at middle Americans. He claimed that in every American town named after a famous city, the locals mangled the pronunciation.

Berlin, Vermont. The locals call it Burr-lin (rhymes with Merlin).

Versailles, Kentucky. The locals call it Ver-sales.

He was traveling through Paris, Tennessee, once with a pack of reporters. "Pull over at that restaurant," he shouted. "I want to prove this once for all."

They went in and walked over to the counter.

"Waddya havin'?" the girl asked.

"Before we order," Kuralt said, "would you tell us the name of the place we're in?"

The girl looked at him as though he was putting her on, or maybe he was just plumb stupid.

"Just pronounce," Kuralt said, slow and precise, "as you always would, the name of the place we're in."

The girl looked at him sideways, leery. And then in a big, sassy Southern drawl, she said, "Dare-ee Qween."

Arrogance, given time, backfires. Often, it's not too serious. We get a little egg on our face, a little bruise on our ego. We wipe it off, marginally humbled.

But sometimes, arrogance is more costly.

The wrath of God is being revealed from heaven against all the godlessness and wickedness of men who suppress the truth by their wickedness, since what may be known about God is plain to them, because God has made it plain to them. For since the creation of the world God's invisible qualities—his eternal power and divine nature—have been clearly seen, being understood from what has been made, so that men are without excuse. For although they knew God, they neither glorified him as God nor gave thanks to him, but their thinking became futile and their foolish hearts were darkened. Although they claimed to be wise, they became fools.... Therefore God gave them over...to sexual impurity for the degrading of their bodies...to shameful lusts...to a depraved mind, to do what ought not to be done.[1]

Sometimes, arrogance is deadly.

❧ ❧ ❧

PULPITS OF LATE HAVE been thin on wrath. We've grown evasive, hesitant, apologetic about it. We prefer a kinder, gentler god. I read a lot of books about God to write this one. Only two addressed the topic of God's wrath straight on, with any kind of backbone. Two others looked at it with sideways, fleeting glances.

Maybe it's a cooling-off period. Maybe for a time we overdid wrath. I've talked to people who grew up, it seems, within earshot of eternal torment, like living next door to the Bastille during the French Revolution. Sunday after Sunday, the preacher, looming vulturelike from the pulpit, breathed out sulfuric fumes, by turns anguishing and gloating over the torments of the damned. These people's childhoods were spent, not singing in the shadow of God's wings, but hiding from the glower of His rage, which sometimes took tangible and personal shape in the form of an angry, abusive parent. Every idle word written down. Every lapse of conduct noted. Every aberrant thought x-rayed.

Singer Butch Hancock described growing up in a church like this. "We were taught two main things: God loves you and He's gonna send you to hell, and sex is bad and nasty and dirty and awful and you should save it for the one you love."[2]

Which raises the real theological conundrum: Is there sex in hell?

Or consider this news item from a few years back:

> JERUSALEM (AP)—One of Israel's most powerful rabbis has ruled that women who wear wigs will be damned. "Both she and her wig will be burned in hell," Rabbi Ovadia Yosef... said in a sermon Saturday. In December 1996, the rabbi decreed that those not respecting the Sabbath should be put to death. He recently declared smoking a sin punishable by forty lashes.[3]

Or consider the story about former Canadian politician Lucien Bouchard, when he was leader of the Quebec separatist movement. One day, the rumor goes, he flew into a fit of anger—stamping on his prosthetic leg like Captain Ahab after Moby Dick evaded him yet again—because his staff served not Arrowroot biscuits, but some other brand for his three o'clock teatime.

Images like that pop into mind for many people when you

mention the wrath of God. They imagine God as a bullying, meddling tyrant, finicky, erupting in curses and diatribes over some petty matter, blistering with vengeance for minor infractions. It's enough to give wrath a bad name.

Other people have hardly *any* conception of God's wrath. If they think of it at all, it is as some vestige of primitive lore, God as archaic, barbaric tribal deity, churlish and fickle, easily provoked. It's an Old Testament thing. The God of Jesus is love.

But Jesus and the writers of the New Testament say more about God's wrath than the Old Testament does. "Do not be afraid of those who kill the body but cannot kill the soul," Jesus said. "Rather, be afraid of the One who can destroy both soul and body in hell."[4] A friend of mine paraphrases this, "Fear Him who, when you're dead, isn't done with you yet."

Likewise, the love of God—a prominent theme in both Testaments—is never kitschy or sentimental. His love is tenacious as oak roots, potent as a typhoon. It is abrasive as much as it is soothing. It scours and breaks us before it sets us right—*in order* to set us right. It never lets us alone. It is so fierce, the love of God, that many choose to be condemned rather than to step out into the light of it. "For God so loved the world," Jesus said, "that he gave his one and only Son, that whoever believes in him shall not perish but have eternal life."[5]

But then He adds:

"This is the verdict: Light has come into the world, but men loved darkness instead of light because their deeds were evil. Everyone who does evil hates the light, and will not come into the light for fear that his deeds will be exposed."[6]

Even the love of God, the light of Christ, holds terror for some.

The wrath of God is not an invention of overzealous preachers. It's not the divine equivalent to an infant's tantrum, a warlord's spree, a tyrant's vengeance. It is real, and it is being revealed, and one day it will be unleashed. We sometimes say, in seasons of havoc and terror, that all hell is breaking loose. But that's nothing. What's truly terrible is when all *heaven* breaks loose. In those days, Jesus says, men will cry out for the rocks to fall on them.

We ignore God's wrath to our own peril. I think of the Greek inventor and mathematician Archimedes. When the Roman general Marcellus invaded his hometown of Syracuse in 212 B.C., Archimedes was outside his house, working on a math problem. The soldiers marched on the city, smashing, burning, looting, killing. Archimedes kept working. They came swift-footed down the street toward him. He sat unaware, immersed in his work. They came upon him and ran him through with a sword. All around him were loud, visible warnings—the thunder of hoof and foot, the clang of sword and spear, the sounds of approaching doom—and he was oblivious until the end.

We ignore God's wrath to our own peril.

SO HOW THEN SHALL WE LIVE? This is for certain: This is a good place to rest, the wrath of God. Truthfully. God's wrath, rightly understood, is one of the most comforting aspects of His character.

Do you really want a God without wrath? Is a God devoid of anger worthy of your worship, your love, your sacrifice? Your trust?

Well, it depends. We've all seen selfish anger. Destructive anger. The anger where a two-hundred-pound man flings a one-hundred-pound woman across the room because she annoys him in some way. The anger where a mother beats her four-year-old for spilling his apple juice, beats him until his back is a relief map of bruises. "A fool," Proverbs says, "gives full vent to his anger."[7] Paul lists "fits of rage" among the deadly sins.[8] "Man's anger," James reminds us, "does not bring about the righteous life that God desires."[9]

We're sickeningly familiar with unholy anger.

But we've also had glimpses of the other kind. Holy anger. I heard recently about a man whose younger brother has

Down's syndrome. One day when they were boys, some kids surrounded his brother and started calling him names, shoving him from one to the other. His round, thickset face grew taut with fear and bewilderment. The older brother, watching this, was at first afraid. But then he got angry, right good and angry. He wasn't physically big, and he was badly outnumbered; but in his anger he grew, and his strength multiplied. He waded in and whipped the whole lot of them.

Stories like that resonate with something clean and deep and noble inside us. We know we are witnessing holy anger. We know, in the face of such things, that anything less than anger would be cowardice. It would be *pusillanimous,* a word whose literal meaning is "small spirit."

Who seeks a pusillanimous god, a god with a shriveled spirit? Who would worship a god who could look out at the world's callous brutality and simply say, "Oh well. Boys will be boys." The police are killing six-year-old children for money in the streets of Rio de Janeiro. Ten-year-old girls are being sold into prostitution in Bangkok. "Oh well"? Who wants a god like that?

Unless the wrath of God is "being revealed from heaven against all the godlessness and wickedness of men," unless it's true that in God there burns a holy anger toward bullies and tyrants and merchants of evil, then He is not God at all. Pusillanimous. His spirit would be too small.

I don't remember my father telling me he loved me until I

was older, almost an adult. He probably did, but I can't recall. He certainly showed me in varied and tangible ways that he loved me—his kibitzing, his manly shoulder-clamping hugs, his handpicked gift at Christmas, usually tucked up far under the tree so that I'd find it last of all. But I remember the first time I was sure of his love, sure enough to rest in it, to let go of feeling I needed to earn it from a paymaster or pry it loose from a closed fist.

It was a time he got so angry that maybe *wrath* is a better word. *Wrath* seems so full-blooded, every last nerve bristling, every bone and sinew awake. He was wrathful, my father.

And it was on my behalf.

My brother and I and some friends were playing street hockey in the wide curve in front of our house, when the neighborhood bully wandered down the street. This was a kid I'd been having some trouble with. He was three years older than me, and big. He'd often wait for me on a pathway I had to walk on my way to and from school. Then he'd shove me, punch me, push me down.

On this occasion, he grabbed my bike and started horsing around on it. I yelled at him to stop. "Make me," he said. I went over. He threw my bike on the ground and then started to thrash me. I fell under the blows.

And then it stopped.

I looked up and saw my oppressor hovering against the sky, but now his face was terror-stricken. My father, who had been watching the bully's antics from our window, had come to my defense. He grabbed the boy by his coat collar and lifted him straight off the ground, like a man hanging from a noose, and shook him.

"Don't you *ever*," my father bellowed, "hurt my son again!"

It was enough. Here was a love I could count on to protect me, to defeat my enemies, to make things right. I basked in that for weeks. His wrath had made my father heroic in my eyes. I could sing in the shadow of his wings.

Strange, but true. I learned to rest in my father's love because of his wrath.

꙳ ꙳ ꙳

BUT WHAT, EXACTLY, is the "godlessness and wickedness" against which God reveals His wrath? In Romans 1, Paul gets down to a lurid and colorful list of godless, wicked things. Idolatry, perversion, greed, envy, depravity. Murder, strife, deceit, malice, gossip. Boastfulness, senselessness, faithlessness, heartlessness, ruthlessness. And the wicked not only do such things but do them *openly*; not in shameful secrecy, but with flaunting brazenness. They even applaud those who invent new vices. As one translation puts it, the wicked "hand out prizes" to those who think up new ways to sin.[10]

Yet it's not quite accurate to say God is angry *about* all this. To be sure, these are godless, wicked things. But God is not revealing His wrath against the acts themselves. Paul's logic is a little more intricate than that. What he actually says is that these acts—perversion, deception, destructiveness—are *symptoms*. They are what people *who are already under God's wrath* turn to, or more precisely, are turned over to.

Three times, Paul says in Romans 1 that wickedness is not the cause of God's anger but the *consequence* of it. God is angry on account of something else—we'll look at what in a minute—and in His anger he has *doomed* people to getting their own way, according to their own desires, their own designs. Wickedness is what they come up with.

Verse 24: *"Therefore, God gave them over...to sexual impurity."*

Verse 26: *"Because of this, God gave them over* to shameful lusts."

Verse 28: *"Furthermore...he gave them over* to a depraved mind."

God's wrath, in its worst and fullest form, is God turning us over. It's God letting us have our own way. *It's God leaving us alone*. And hell is God's way of letting us have our own way in His absence for eternity. The lost, C. S. Lewis said, "enjoy forever the horrible freedom they have demanded."[11]

Proverbs says and Hebrews repeats, "My son, do not make light of the Lord's discipline, and do not lose heart when he rebukes you, because the Lord disciplines those he loves, and he punishes everyone he accepts as a son."[12] When God's anger reaches the level of wrath, it turns out He doesn't start punishing us.

He stops.

He shows His wrath, but not by thrashing us. It's worse. He shows it by abandoning us, leaving us all to ourselves.

At least, this is the primary manifestation of His wrath now, while there is still daylight. Another time is coming—the prophets call it the great and terrible day of the Lord—when God will punish all wickedness, when He will pull and gather and burn the tares. There is a day when all that is evil will be *herem,* the Hebrew word meaning the utter destruction of things too wicked to be redeemed. Jericho was made *herem.* Except for one woman and her family who turned to the light, all else was removed by sword and fire.

As I write, a horrible event unfolds in eastern Canada, in a suburb of Toronto. A ten-year-old girl was abducted from her own yard. The next day, her arm and leg washed up on the shores of Lake Ontario.

The killer is on the loose.

The killer may be caught. The killer may not. But even if he (or she or they) is, can justice ever be done on earth? *Can man's anger bring about the righteous life God desires?*

Only God can do that. Only His wrath can minister justice in a way that *shalom* comes in its wake. We wait for that great and terrible day of the Lord when all evil is *herem.*

But for now, for the most part, God just turns the unrepentantly wicked over.

❧ ❧ ❧

IF WICKEDNESS IS THE consequence of God's wrath, what is the cause? What initially sparks God's anger? What is the root sin, the molten core of wickedness and godlessness, that convinces God to turn us over?

It's thanklessness.

> The wrath of God is being revealed from heaven against all the godlessness and wickedness of men who suppress the truth by their wickedness, since what may be known about God is plain to them, because God has made it plain to them. For since the creation of the world God's invisible qualities—his eternal power and divine nature—have been clearly seen, being understood from what has been made, so that men are without excuse. For although they knew God, they neither glorified him as God nor gave thanks to him, but their thinking became futile and their foolish hearts were darkened.[13]

For although they knew God, they neither glorified Him as God nor gave thanks to Him. The heart of wickedness and godlessness is the refusal to glorify God. It's the failure to thank Him.

Which, frankly, doesn't seem so bad.

Or does it?

I was in Uganda, Africa, about a dozen years ago, in a little township called Wairaka. Every Sunday evening, about one hundred Christians from the neighboring area would gather to worship. They met at the edge of a cornfield, under a lean-to with a rusty tin roof that cracked like gunfire when it rained. They sat—when they did sit—on rough wood benches. The floor was dirt. The band's instruments were old or handmade—bruised, scratched guitars with corroded strings and necks that had warped in the humidity; a plinky electric piano plugged into a crackling speaker; shakers made of tin cans and stones. All of it kept straying out of tune.

One Sunday evening, I was too sour to join in. The music sounded squawky. I was miffed at someone on our missions team. I found the food bland, tasteless. I was feeling deprived and misunderstood. I found the joy of others hollow, mustered-up. I was miserable, and I wanted to wallow in it.

The pastor asked if anyone had anything to share. Many people wanted to, but a tall, willowy woman in the back row danced and shouted loudest, so he called her forward. She came twirling her long limbs, trilling out praise.

"Oh, brothers and sisters, I love Jesus so much," she said.

"Tell us, sister! Tell us!" the Ugandans shouted back.

"Oh, I love Him so much, I don't know where to begin. He is so good to me. Where do I begin to tell you how good He is to me?"

"Begin there, sister! Begin right there!"

"Oh," she said, "He is so good. I praise Him all the time for how good He is. For three months, I prayed to Him for shoes. And look!" And with that the woman cocked up her leg so that we could see one foot. One very ordinary shoe covered it. "He gave me shoes."

The Ugandans went wild. They clapped, they cheered, they whistled, they yelled.

But not me. I was devastated. I sat there broken and grieving. In an instant, God snapped me out of my self-pity and plunged me into repentance. In all my life, I had not once prayed for shoes. It never even crossed my mind. And in all my life, I had not even once thanked God for the many, many shoes I had.

Thanklessness becomes its own prison. Persisted in, it becomes its own hell, where there is outer darkness and gnashing of teeth. Thanklessness is the place God doesn't dwell, the place that, if we inhabit it too often, He turns us over to. "See to it that no one misses the grace of God," Hebrews says, "and that no bitter root grows up to cause trouble and defile many."[14] Thanklessness troubles and defiles many, because first it troubles and defiles the one in whom bitterness takes root.

God's wrath is revealed, before anything, against thanklessness. All the wickedness in the world begins with an act of forgetting. God shows Himself, but we forget and are defiled.

NOW I HAVE GRIM NEWS. God has turned all of us over.

That's what Paul concludes in Romans: "What shall we conclude then? Are we ["moral" people] any better [than "immoral" people]? Not at all! [We] are all under sin."[15] Every one of us is under the wrath of God, in danger of God's wrath. None of us has fully thanked Him.

But there's also good news, great good news.

Jesus has come to cover over our sin: "God demonstrates his own love for us in this: While we were still sinners [under the wrath of God] Christ died for us. Since we have now been justified by his blood, how much more shall we be saved from God's wrath through him!"[16]

We wait for God's "Son from heaven, whom [God] raised from the dead—Jesus, who rescues us from the coming wrath."[17]

So we come to this: We can rest in the wrath of God, knowing that God is just and acts justly, but only after we rest in the forgiveness of God through Jesus Christ, for we have all fallen short of the glory of God.

In the pioneer days on the prairie lands, people sometimes would find themselves about to be consumed. They would be in the middle of a field and a fire would catch in the tall, dry grass. Stiff winds pushed the flames toward them, so fast not even horses could outrun them. There was no time to escape. Instead, they took a match and burned a patch of ground where they stood. Then they waited on the burned-over earth. The prairie fire swept up to the edge of the patch and, finding nothing there to consume, passed by.

And later the fire proved a gift to the earth: It burned what was already dead, and its ashes nurtured new life.

Jesus Christ burned the earth with His cross. God poured out His wrath on His Son. If we take our stand there, the wrath to come will pass us by, and in its time will renew the very earth it devours.

Don't even try to run.

Just rest there, thankful.

Chapter Six

THE INNKEEPER'S ROOM

God's Mercy

A man was talking to a book collector. The collector sought and savored rare tomes; he loved their musty, brittle pages, their ragged edges, the engraved lettering on the covers, rubbed almost smooth from countless hands. "I once found an old Bible in my grandfather's attic," the man told the collector, just making idle conversation. "Somebody named Guttenberg had printed it."

"Guttenberg!" the collector said. "Where is it now?"

"Oh, I tossed it out. It was really old, not much use."

"Do you realize what you've done? That was one of the first Bibles ever printed. One copy auctions for $2 million."

"Ah," the man said, "not mine. Mine wouldn't have fetched more than a buck or two. I couldn't even read the bleedin' thing. Some idiot named Martin Luther had scribbled all over it."

The story is a bit of whimsy, but it captures a bitter truth: Sometimes we treat precious things as worthless things. We see treasures as clutter, because we're ignorant of their true value.

We do that even with words. Words that were once to us like elixir—the stuff of everlasting youth—are now to us like soda pop—cheap, common, leeching nourishment from our bones. Words that were once to us as jewels—rare and costly—are now to us like stones—common and expendable. We toss them about carelessly. We trample them, kick them, and leave them where they lie. There are many words we do that with. *Love. Holiness. Hope. Salvation.*

And this. *Mercy.*

Mercy is a precious thing we've come to treat as a worthless thing.

Blame Roy Orbison. On his 1964 hit single "Oh, Pretty Woman," Orbison growls and purrs the word—*Mercyyyy!*— making it by turns a seduction, a taunt, a joke. But I think we lost mercy's value much earlier. I think it started the day we first saw ourselves as basically good people—in need of a pep talk now and then, a shot in the arm, maybe. But *mercy?* Mercy's for criminals. Mercy's for beggars. Mercy's for bankrupts.

It's for people in a ditch.

I ONCE MET A YOUNG MAN who refused to picture his grandmother in a ditch. He understood that bad people need mercy—but not his *grandmother,* who baked cookies and mended torn clothes and crocheted doilies and nursed his grandfather through a series of strokes that worsened, with each one, his dementia and belligerence, until finally he was like a gored bull. And she did it all with grace. But she had never shown the slightest interest in God.

"So is she going to hell?" he asked.

I started to quote the Bible. "All have sinned and fallen short of the glory of God..."

"Yeah, yeah, I know," he said. "I just don't understand why she forfeits heaven, and some rabid serial murderer can repent and the doors fly open."

I sat there, stumped. I whittled out some spindly answer that supported exactly nothing and satisfied neither of us. He left, embarrassed for me and still angry.

Later it occurred to me that Jesus once had a similar conversation with another young man. *Who needs mercy?* That was the conversation's underlying question. Jesus answered it, but not with weighty theological pronouncements or flimsy evangelical slogans.

He told a story.

A man travels to Jericho. That's a bad road, full of bad

characters, and not surprisingly, the man gets mugged. The brigands beat him, rob him, strip him, and hurl him in a ditch, leaving him crumpled, naked, and very, very pale. Someone must act. Someone must have mercy, or the man will die. But who?

A Priest?

No.

A Levite?

No.

A Samaritan?

Yes.

A Samaritan. The hated Samaritans, rumor has it, are stingy and spiteful, and maybe not altogether *there*. These are people from whom no one expects mercy.

But this Samaritan defies all expectations. He draws near. He touches the man's wounds. He cleans and bandages him and carries him to safety. He pays an innkeeper to nurse him back to health, and offers to come back and pay any more that's owed.

It's a story, obviously, about mercy. A man—a despised outsider—shows mercy to a stranger in a ditch.

"Go," Jesus says, to end the tale, "and do likewise."

Meaning what? That I'm to *show* mercy? Or that I'm to *receive* mercy?

Obviously I need to back up.

This parable, like so many Jesus tells, comes in response to a question.

On one occasion an expert in the law stood up to test Jesus. "Teacher," he asked, "what must I do to inherit eternal life?"

"What is written in the Law?" he replied. "How do you read it?"

He answered: "'Love the Lord your God with all your heart and with all your soul and with all your strength and with all your mind'; and, 'Love your neighbor as yourself.'"

"You have answered correctly," Jesus replied. "Do this and you will live."

But he wanted to justify himself, so he asked Jesus, "And who is my neighbor?"[1]

But he wanted to justify himself. So Jesus tells the young man this story about a Samaritan who shows mercy. But watch how the dialogue ends.

Jesus asks, "Which of these three do you think was a neighbor to the man who fell into the hands of robbers?"

The expert in the law replies, "The one who had mercy on him."[2]

The neighbor is the one *who has mercy.*

Did you catch that? My neighbor isn't someone I have mercy upon—*it's someone who has mercy on me.*

Which means I'm the one in need of mercy.

I'm the one in the ditch.

This expert in the law is convinced of his own goodness. He believes he can *do* things to inherit eternal life, if he just knows what they are. He desires to *justify* himself. *If I'm to love my neighbor, just show me my neighbor, and let me at him.*

But Jesus subverts him. He defines his neighbor as the man who *loves him,* the one who *has mercy on him.* His neighbor is the one who finds him slumped and bloody in a ditch, lifts him out, and pays for it all.

Go and do likewise. Go discover how desperate, naked, and left for dead you really are. Go discover that you are, in fact, broken and lying in a ditch. Go discover that there is no way to justify yourself. Go discover that you can't *do* a single thing to inherit eternal life, that unless Someone has mercy on you—extravagant, sacrificial mercy—yes, unless the God of the Holy Wild happens by, a jar brimming with oil in hand, and pockets stuffed with coins to pay the innkeeper, and He stops—well, you're as good as dead.

What must I do to inherit eternal life? Simple: Realize I'm in a ditch. Realize that I'm doomed unless my Neighbor loves me. Realize I need mercy as much as I need to give it.

Go and do likewise.

THE LONGER I LIVE, the more I crave it anyhow, mercy.

A cartoon shows a husband and wife standing in a long,

curving line before the gates of heaven. They're waiting for their turn to face judgment. The woman leans toward the man and whispers behind her hand, "Now, Harold, whatever you do, please don't demand what's coming to you."

I understand that a little better every year.

I grew up outside the church. I was an expert in lawlessness, not the Law, and so I instinctively knew not to demand what was coming to me. I needed mercy. I still wanted to justify myself, still wanted to do something to inherit eternal life. But deep down I knew something quite different was called for. I was mortally wounded—in the ditch by my own choice—and God had to pour out oil and wine on me, or else I was as good as dead.

What surprises me, twenty-some years later, is that mercy is my daily portion. I haven't outgrown my hunger or my need for it. If anything, both have increased. Micah asks what God requires of us and then answers three things: to do justly, to love mercy, and to walk humbly with our God. What Micah doesn't say explicitly—I had to figure this one out on my own—is that the love of mercy grows naturally from the practice of justice and the discipline of walking with God. It grows naturally, because these things daily expose our need for mercy. The attempt to walk humbly and do justly, at least in my own case, has uncovered the wiliness of my own heart, the cunning and tenacity of my sloth, my thousand cheap disguises, my endless excuses. It's revealed how what I call justice is often only self-protection, self-vindication, raw spite. It's shown me how hard—how nearly impossible—it is to walk humbly and to do justly.

So I love mercy.

I think this is the place Paul came to as an old man, and if I've arrived at the place sooner than him, it's only because he held my hand and led me there. Early on, writing his opuses to the Ephesians and Romans, Paul said some remarkable things about the mercy of God. "God has bound all men over to disobedience so that he *may have mercy on them all,*" he declared to the Romans.[3] "Because of his great love for us," he announced to the Ephesians, "God, *who is rich in mercy,* made us alive with Christ even when we were dead in transgressions."[4]

These things are true. But they still come off as creedal formula, lofty doctrinal pronouncements. Such things are the $E=mc^2$ of Christian theology. They disclose the hidden springs and levers of the cosmos, what makes it hum and tick and hold together. But even though we are bound up intimately, moment by moment, in their reality, we don't always feel in these passages that reality pressing into us, hot against our skin, burning and urgent and cleansing.

Mercy seems here merely theoretical: God is merciful, ineffable, impassable....

I doubt it was ever this for Paul. God caught him up by the scruff of his stiff neck, and he never forgot it. He never lapsed into hairsplitting quibbles or dry speculations. And yet, not until he's much older, hobbling from years of hardship, virtually tattooed with scars, does his voice take on a rich personal tone when he speaks of mercy.

"Here is a trustworthy saying that deserves full acceptance," he writes to Timothy. "Christ Jesus came into the world to save sinners—of whom I am the worst. But for that very reason *I was shown mercy* so that in me, the worst of sinners, Christ Jesus might display his unlimited patience as an example for those who would believe on him and receive eternal life."[5]

Paul loves mercy.

I sometimes wonder if a soldier of fortune could have hurt more people than I have as a father and husband and pastor. I had no idea when I said "I do" to my wife, or brought each of my three children home from the hospital, or said yes to the churches that called me, that these things would bring in their wake, along with much joy, much *pain*—the thousand ways I could miss, could wound, could rob and leave in ditches the very people I love deeply.

I had no idea how gut-wrenching it is to remove a friend from church membership because, though you shake him and plead with him and weep for him, he won't quit the sin he's in. I had no idea how sharp and septic it cuts when someone you've broken bread with walks away, angry and bitter, refusing to speak with you. I had no idea how alone and betrayed and bewildered and weary you could feel in your most intimate relationships.

But I know now. And with each new gain in this terrible knowing, I grow hungrier for mercy.

As a young man, Paul saw mercy as God's gift to all humanity, a rainfall that fell on the withering land. And it is. But late in his years, he saw something else besides: God's mercy as Christ's unlimited patience *toward him,* the worst of sinners, a cup of cold water held to his parched lips, day after day after day.

And I think King David knew this in his bones as well, this deep, wide, rich mercy of God. And like Paul, he knew it best late in life. After David has survived years of rebellion and betrayal—his own and others'—the kingdom is thriving again. This is after David's adultery with Bathsheba, after his coolly calculated murder of Uriah, after the death of his newborn son, after his eldest son, Absalom, rebelled and was killed. This is after the trysts and court intrigues and palace coups, after sorrow upon sorrow, desolation upon desolation. After all that, there comes again a season of peace. Order and power and prosperity descend on David's life and his kingdom.

And David forgets. He forgets where it comes from, where *he's* come from, what he's been through. He forgets how costly self-reliance is. And forgetting, he does a foolish thing. He indulges in a bit of chest-swelling, a bit of strutting, a bit of trophy-flaunting.

David counts his fighting men.

This seems a small thing. But for David, it is a major act

of defiance and pride. For David, it's faithlessness. As David sang so often in his psalms, God has always been his rock and fortress, a shield about him, the God who delivers him. David has always been the one who goes up against giants wearing only a tunic, carrying only stones. God is with him. God goes before him. He's never had to fear the thousands drawn up against him, the tens of thousands gathered around.

God fights David's battles.

But now David counts his fighting men.

Even Joab, David's cunning, conniving war general who always seemed to find David's piety a tad naive, warns David against the idea: "May the LORD your God multiply the troops a hundred times over, and may the eyes of my lord the king see it. But why does my lord the king want to do such a thing?"[6]

But David blunders on. And only after it's done, nearly ten months later, after he's got his number, does he wake up to what he's done.

> David was conscience-stricken after he had counted the fighting men, and he said to the LORD, "I have sinned greatly in what I have done. Now, O LORD, I beg you, take away the guilt of your servant. I have done a very foolish thing."[7]

But there are consequences.

Before David got up the next morning, the word of the LORD had come to Gad the prophet, David's seer: "Go and tell David, 'This is what the LORD says: I am giving you three options. Choose one of them for me to carry out against you.'"

So Gad went to David and said to him, "Shall there come upon you three years of famine in your land? Or three months of fleeing from your enemies while they pursue you? Or three days of plague in your land? Now then, think it over and decide how I should answer the one who sent me."[8]

It's David's response that gets me: "I am in deep distress. Let us fall into the hands of the LORD, *for his mercy is great*; but do not let me fall into the hands of men."[9]

David knew where to rest. He would run to the Holy Wild every time. David knew that in God's hands, he might be crushed, but he'd be safer there than anywhere. In God's hands, the breaking of the bone and the mending of it, the making of the wound and the healing of it, come joined. God's mercy might be severe. But it never ceases being mercy.

Always, let me fall into God's hands.

To LOVE MERCY. God Himself loves it. He has, A. W. Tozer said, put a safety lock on His wrath, but a hair trigger on His mercy.

Maybe you've heard the story of one church's Christmas Sunday school pageant. The older class was performing the Nativity, but they had a problem. One of the boys, Alf, was thick in head and tongue. He mangled lines, mauled scenes. But he badly wanted to be in the play. So the teacher cast him as the innkeeper. This was safe. Foolproof.

All Alf had to do was turn Joseph and Mary away.

He had a single line: "Go away!" He had a single gesture: a brusque, backward sweep of the arm, a motion of refusal and rejection. He practiced and practiced, and Alf got it down pretty good.

The night of the pageant arrives. Here come Joseph and Mary, moving slowly, coats pulled tight around their shoulders, Mary's stomach bulging with child. Alf stands at the innkeeper's door, glowering with menace, and Joseph pleads with him, "Please, sir, my wife is having a baby! Have you room at the inn?"

"Go away!" Alf booms. Perfect. He sweeps the air with a violent, dismissive gesture. Again, perfect. He slams the door shut.

Perfect.

Joseph and Mary turn to leave.

But then the door opens again. Mary and Joseph turn and look. There's the innkeeper, there's Alf, weeping, shaking his big, thick head. He cups his hand and curls back his arm toward himself, gesturing for them to approach.

"You can come in," he says. "I changed my mind. You can have my room."

Mercy is God going and doing likewise.

"Come in," He says. "I've changed My mind. You can have My room."

> Praise be to the God and Father of our Lord Jesus Christ! In his great mercy he has given us new birth into a living hope through the resurrection of Jesus Christ from the dead, and into an inheritance that can never perish, spoil or fade—kept in heaven for you.[10]

Who is my neighbor? The One who found me in a ditch and didn't pass by, who saw me without shelter and gave me His room.

Even your grandmother needs that.

Chapter Seven

WHERE THE LAMB IS SLAIN

God's Victory

Lambs are such soft creatures, spindly-legged, timid. The very symbol of vulnerability. When my children and I go to petting zoos, we seek out the lambs for their shy curiosity, their skittishness, their simpleminded trust, their utter neediness. We fill our hands with pellets of food and laugh at the way their warmish, coolish noses tickle the skin on our palms as they eat.

You always want to protect a lamb.

But follow one? Worship one? Entrust your deepest treasures to one? Rest in the triumph of one? Believe that a lamb leads the way in the Holy Wild?

The book of Revelation says so. John's vision depicts the enthroned Jesus, the One who receives the worship of all creation, who presides over the drama and consummation of all history, who leads the armies of heaven in vanquishing all evil, who ushers in all the glories of paradise—he depicts this One as "a Lamb, looking as if it had been slain."[1]

It defies all sense.

The 1986 film *The Mission* tells the story of Jesuit missionaries working in the jungle highlands of Brazil—mountainous, cavernous, perilous terrain, a land that entangles and devours. They've risked all to bring the gospel to the people who live hidden in the folds and shadows of that lush earth. The Holy Wild indeed. It's work you must be prepared to give your life for, literally: Tribal warriors skewered the first missionaries clean through, sent their bodies floating down river and hurtling over a waterfall, a warning to all who would dare follow. But they followed anyhow. God's fools. And their stubbornness has won out. The entire tribe has converted and been baptized in the very waters once used as pallbearer.

The Lamb, it seems, has conquered.

The closing scene of the movie begins as a day of celebration. The men and women who once hated these missionaries stand alongside them now. Together, they have built a new church. They are marching in joyful procession to the house of the Lord, to enter in, to worship. It is the crowning moment of years of prayer and sacrifice.

The priest at the head of the procession raises up a cross and begins the march through the jungle. But suddenly other men appear, white men, men who have been crouching low among pampas grass, in thickets, in shadows. Men with guns. Men with cannons. Men with hate.

Men who have come to destroy.

The scene is played in agonizing, mesmerizing slowness. The priests and the people walk stately, serene. They sing a hymn of praise.

Fire and smoke spew from gun barrels, belch from cannons. Earth and blood mingle. A torch is thrown on the thatch of the newly built church, and it erupts in bright flame and collapses in black smoke. One by one, the Christians go down, their limbs twisting beneath the weight of their falling bodies.[2]

The Lamb, it seems, is conquered.

Has conquered. Is conquered. Which is it?

⁂

"ALL AUTHORITY IN HEAVEN and on earth has been given to me," Jesus said. The apostle Paul agrees: "Having disarmed the powers and authorities...[Christ] made a public spectacle of them, triumphing over them."[3]

In 1939, the year Hitler mobilized for war in Europe, Helmut Thielicke was ordained as a pastor and given his first church in Germany. Thielicke arrived with youthful boldness, believing Jesus' words, "All authority in heaven and on earth has been given to me." He told himself that Hitler was a pathetic little puppet, dangling on thin strings.

He called for a Bible study. Three people showed up—two ancient women, brittle and crepe-skinned, and a man, even older, who played the organ with shaking hands. Huddled together in their little church, they could hear, just outside, the sound of thousands of jackboots, hard as hammers, rhythmic as pistons, striking the pavement. It was Hitler's Youth Corps, out marching.

And the young, brash Thielicke's confidence broke.

All power?

Thielicke realized, as most of us at some point come to realize, that either Jesus' words held a depth of meaning he had yet to glimpse or grasp, or that His words were utterly hollow, devoid of substance, words of reckless exaggeration and empty boast. A lamb masquerading as a lion.

The Bible teaches that God will triumph at the end of the ages. This we can believe. Indeed, our hope is pinned on it. But the Bible also teaches that God has triumphed here, now.

Which stretches credibility. Does any claim seem more preposterous?

Behold God's visible kingdom on earth: you, me, Aunt Mildred, and that eccentric, muttering man who can never button his shirts straight, get that cowlick tamed, scrub out the food crusted in his mustache, or mask his acrid, sweaty smell. We often resemble, despite our veneer of robustness, Thielicke's Bible study group—frail, huddled, startled by the jackboots striking the pavement. We often look like David when he hid from Saul—promised the kingdom at some undisclosed point in the future, but for now a vagabond, a fugitive, a scavenger. Even thriving churches—great, bustling, metropolis-like churches—can hardly be accused, as Paul and Silas were in Thessalonica, of turning the world "upside down."[4]

Yet the Bible insists: *We are more than conquerors.*[5]

How so?

Well, to start, this: Victory, God-style, almost always looks like a defeat in the making, a catastrophe brewing. It has a lamb-like quality about it.

As with Gideon. Gideon's story is found in the early pages of Judges, in the Old Testament. Gideon, when we first meet him, is a timid man, cowering from the marauding Midianites, hiding out in the mountains. He's the runt of the lowest clan. He's like a lamb.

But God doesn't see things that way. He calls Gideon "mighty warrior," and directs him to lead an attack against the Midianites.

So Gideon, after some balking and dodging, assembles a rough rabble of farmers and peasants numbering about thirty-two thousand. They come with plowshares sharpened into spears, with sticks, with slingshots. It's not very impressive. The Midianites are skilled and ruthless warriors. They have state-of-the-art weaponry. They have a cavalry of camel riders. They have one hundred and thirty-five thousand fighting men. They're spoiling for a fight, and they're good at it.

And God tells Gideon he has too many men.

Too many. God tells Gideon to send the fearful ones home. Twenty-two thousand leave, and ten thousand stay. God tells Gideon he still has too many. Gideon sifts them out again, this time on the basis of how they drink water from a brook. By the time he's done, only three hundred men remain. Three hundred men against one hundred and thirty-five thousand Midianites. Then God tells Gideon one thing more: Take no weapons. Each man is to go up against the enemy bearing only a torch, a clay jar, and a horn.

And the three hundred win.[6]

Which is the story of the Cross. All principalities and powers are arrayed against God. Satan, the commanding general of the enemy forces, has the whole thing wrapped up. He has the ultimate weapon, the final solution: Kill Jesus.

The devil has everyone bound over to sin and death. Long ago, on a cool morning in a sun-dappled garden, Satan made sure of that. He's been making sure of it ever since.

But there's this one threat: this skinny carpenter who's been walking around Galilee and Jerusalem. He's been preaching, healing, touching lepers, confronting hypocrites, telling stories. *Forgiving people their sins*. He must be dealt with, decisively.

Satan's done a great job so far. He's covered all the angles. He's won all the power brokers over to his side. He's provoked the Romans to action. He's drawn together the warring factions of the Jewish establishment—the Herodians, the Sadducees, the priests, the Pharisees—and that's no small achievement. He's worked them over well, made them feel betrayed, disappointed, resentful, vengeful. Everyone agrees: Jesus must go.

All Satan needs now is the Man.

And, talk about luck, here He comes, walking straight at them. Not a weapon on Him. His silly little army—fishermen, tax collectors, a few old whores—bumble along and soon abandon Him.

He's all alone. Vulnerable. Pitiable, almost. He doesn't put up any struggle. Next thing you know, there's Jesus, His body cut and swollen with whip blows. Next thing you know, the Romans are nailing Him to a cross, flinging Him up mangled and dangling against a dark sky.

Like a lamb to the slaughter.

Next thing you know, He's dead.

It is finished.

Only, what's finished? Who's finished? *Having disarmed the powers and authorities, He made a public spectacle of them, triumphing over them by the Cross.* The very thing that looked like defeat turned into triumph.

Paul invokes an image here of a Roman general returning home victorious. He's conquered, triumphed. He parades through the streets in dazzling pageantry, his bedraggled and shackled captives staggering behind him. Satan thought this was him, the conquering general, Jesus his ruined and tethered captive.

But exactly the opposite happened. The Cross was the devil's Trojan horse, the gift he seized that undid him. He thought it was his weapon to secure his power. It turned out to be God's weapon to destroy it. "The reason the Son of God appeared," John declares, "was to destroy the devil's work."[7] John describes the devil's work as sin's grip on us, its death grip.

The Cross broke that.

It is finished.

❧ ❧ ❧

OR IS IT? The jackboots still hammer the pavement, in one place or another, undiminished it appears. The devil, at one time or another, still taunts and struts, undaunted it seems. Why is God's triumph not more visible? Why does it seem so rickety and piecemeal? And maybe more troubling than that, why do the followers of the Lamb, reputedly more than conquerors, so often look defeated? Sin still crouches at our doors, desiring to have us. Why hasn't God conquered, not just the *penalty of sin,* but also its menace, its grip, its power?

The best I can answer is this: Christ still conquers through the Cross. His victory is still won as a lamb to the slaughter. In fact, what is different now is that every day we also enter into that paradoxical conquest: We take up our cross and follow Him. We enter into God's victory, His once-for-all and yet presently unfolding victory, through the doorway of our own suffering and dying. We rest in God's victory, not through brashness, but through meekness. Not by gloating, but by surrender. The shape of our triumph is still cruciform.

It's still lamblike.

The book of Revelation portrays God's final and utter victory. He vanquishes death, sickness, evil, the evil one. But even Revelation primarily reminds us that Christ overcomes the world, not by swords, nor legislation, nor power blocs or lobby groups or protest rallies.

He does it by the Cross.

Chapter 12 of Revelation paints a lurid picture of the devil's mayhem. Satan is an enraged, engorged dragon, devouring, destroying. The church and her saints overcome him by "the blood of the Lamb and by the word of their testimony." They defeat him because they do not "love their lives so much as to shrink from death."[8] *The shape of their triumph is cruciform.* They take up their cross and follow like lambs to the slaughter, and by that they overcome.

It's three hundred men with clay jars and torches, bleating their horns in the dark, while just beyond, a vast army of destroyers clutch their broadswords and rise.

God has always triumphed this way, by His blood and the words of His martyrs, by Gideon's clay jars and torchlight.

Like Telemachus.

Telemachus was a monk and a pig farmer in fifth-century Asia Minor. Small, wiry, and shy, he was a simple man, and simpleminded. But God spoke to him and told him that he was to go to Rome and bring an end to the popular blood-sport, the games of the gladiators. Telemachus did what he was told, setting out on foot for the long journey. He had no plan, just a word from God. He arrived in Rome and went to the Colosseum. Men were bludgeoning and hewing one another with swords and pikes and maces. The crowd roared their approval. Telemachus moved among the crowd, yelling in his shrill voice for this to stop. The people, the few that heard him, laughed. They threw things at him.

So he jumped down onto the floor of the Colosseum, flailing, shouting, pleading. More jeered him, threw things at him.

Then someone threw a stone. And another, and another. They threw stones until the monk's small, shattered body slumped to the ground, and the earth turned dark with his blood. A lamb to the slaughter.

Then the crowd woke up. Holy dread fell on them, and a harrowing silence. One man stood and walked out. Then two, three, ten, a hundred. A thousand. All. They walked out. No one ever came back.[9]

It was finished.

By the blood of the Lamb and by the word of his testimony, not loving his life so much as to shrink from death.

The Lamb still conquers by the Cross.

ैँँ ैँ ैँ

EVEN THE RESURRECTION is a triumph in a way we least expect. The risen Christ comes into a locked room where His disciples are meeting. Thomas is there. Thomas won't believe Jesus is risen unless he sees it with his own eyes. He won't believe Jesus has triumphed—over sin, over death, over the devil—until he sees Christ alive, vigorous, breathing, His flesh supple and warm and blood-hued.

And so Jesus comes to him.

Imagine it was you proving your victory to Thomas. What sign would you bring? I might bring Herod's head on a platter. Or the high priest in shackles, his beard torn out. Or Pilate, raw from a whipping.

Or maybe I'd do stunts. Maybe, to taunt the devil for his gall, I'd at long last avenge myself for those temptations. I'd turn stones to bread, leap from the temple and have angels catch me, flaunt my dominion over all the kingdoms of the world. I'd show that I'd won the prize, and without his help.

Something like that.

Jesus shows Thomas His wounds.

God's triumph comes disguised. Wounds, words, blood, clay jars. Paul knew that. He wrote:

> What, then, shall we say in response to this?
> If God is for us, who can be against us? He

who did not spare his own Son, but gave him up for us all—how will he not also, along with him, graciously give us all things? Who will bring any charge against those whom God has chosen? It is God who justifies. Who is he that condemns? Christ Jesus, who died—more than that, who was raised to life—is at the right hand of God and is also interceding for us. Who shall separate us from the love of Christ? Shall trouble or hardship or persecution or famine or nakedness or danger or sword? As it is written:

"For your sake we face death all day long; we are considered as sheep to be slaughtered."

No, in all these things we are more than conquerors through him who loved us. For I am convinced that neither death nor life, neither angels nor demons, neither the present nor the future, nor any powers, neither height nor depth, nor anything else in all creation, will be able to separate us from the love of God that is in Christ Jesus our Lord.[10]

Trouble, hardship, persecution, famine, nakedness, danger, sword—*in all these things, we are more than conquerors.*

In all these things. The triumph comes disguised. Because in the midst of the devil's mayhem, the dragon's rampage, the thunder of his vast army's jackboots, there's a cross. And the Cross does every time what power and might is impotent to do: It destroys the work of the devil. Because that work is always, everywhere, one thing only in the end: to separate you, me, all of us, from God's love.

The assassination of Martin Luther King Jr. threatened to sabotage and undermine all the gains of the civil rights movement. The movement was fragile anyhow, fissured and patchy, many of its leaders compromised, its foot soldiers demoralized. King's death brought all of that to a head. In some ways, his funeral was more than a burial service for King—it had the potential to be the burial service for the movement.

There was a large roster of speakers, eulogizers, exhorters. But one stood out: James Bevel. He mounted the podium, stern and heavy, and in a voice like a storm gathering at the far edge of a clear day, he said, "There is false rumor going around that our leader is dead. Our leader is not dead. Martin Luther King is not our leader." At this he paused and let his words, the implications of his words, sting, stir, taunt, bruise. Was he using this moment to loose a political hornet's nest, to make havoc in the ranks?

"Our leader," Bevel continued, "is the Man who led Moses out of Israel."

"Thass the man!" someone yelled.

"Our leader is the Man who went with Daniel into the lion's den."

"Same man!"

"Our leader is the Man who walked out of the grave on Easter morning. Our leader neither sleeps nor slumbers. He cannot be put in jail. He has never lost a war yet. Our leader is still on the case. Our leader is not dead. One of His prophets died. We will not stop because of that."[11]

Our leader is not dead.

The Lamb just keeps conquering by the Cross.

❧ ❧ ❧

ON NOVEMBER 27, 1989, a spontaneous celebration burst out all over Czechoslovakia. Communism had fallen, its squat monuments sprawled facedown in the dust, children dancing atop them. Little old ladies, prisoners, pig farmers, dock-workers—all had prayed for this day for a long time. They had suffered for it. Many had died for it.

Now it was here. Now it was finished.

Church bells had been silent in that country for forty-five years. But on that day, at high noon, every church bell in the country bonged and clanged. Pigeons, startled, scattered from the belfries in thousands, a blur of white and gray across the sky. The people, amazed, let out a shout of joy so loud it almost drowned the music.

On a lawn in front of a church in Prague, someone staked a sign: *The Lamb Wins!*

One day, Christ will return. Not on a donkey, weeping. Not on a cross, dying. But on a stallion, a sword coming from His mouth, conquering as He comes. On that day, *every* knee *will* bow and *every* tongue *will* confess that He is Lord.

Between then and now, though, the dragon rages, the jackboots hammer, the devil dances. The victory comes disguised. Words. Blood. Wounds. Clay jars. Torchlight.

But rest in this: He's still on the case, and not one thing anywhere can separate you from His love.

The Lamb wins.

Chapter Eight

THE PRESENCE OF RUIN

God's Holiness

I n the year that King Uzziah died, I saw the Lord seated on a throne, high and exalted, and the train of his robe filled the temple. Above him were seraphs, each with six wings: With two wings they covered their faces, with two they covered their feet, and with two they were flying. And they were calling to one another:

> "Holy, holy, holy is the LORD Almighty;
> the whole earth is full of his glory."

At the sound of their voices the doorposts and thresholds shook and the temple was filled with smoke.

"Woe to me!" I cried. "I am ruined! For I am a man of unclean lips, and I live among a people of unclean lips, and my eyes have seen the King, the Lord Almighty."

Then one of the seraphs flew to me with a live coal in his hand, which he had taken with tongs from the altar. With it he touched my mouth and said, "See, this has touched your lips; your guilt is taken away and your sin atoned for."

Then I heard the voice of the Lord saying, "Whom shall I send? And who will go for us?"

And I said, "Here am I. Send me!"[1]

The king is dead.

Uzziah has been a good king, as kings go. He came to the throne young, at sixteen, a sapling only, gangly and flute-voiced, feather-boned, unsteady. And he landed in a quagmire of political turmoil. Yet he triumphed. During his fifty-two-year reign, he ushered in peace and prosperity. He took control of the sea and undertook great building projects. He routed out the Philistines and subdued the Ammonites.

Uzziah had held the feared Assyrians at bay. He had thwarted, over and over, the bloodlust of the their warrior king, Tiglath-Pileser. Tiglath-Pileser's armies, like Saruman's orcs, were bred to destroy. This was their pleasure. They were well-armed and well-organized marauders, a vast and disciplined regiment of vandals and arsonists. They reduced towns to rubble, temples to char, kings to beggars, princes to slaves.

But not Uzziah. Not Judah. Not Jerusalem. Tiglath-Pileser wanted to conquer here, too. His army prowled the edges, scratching at the door, bellowing threats. But Uzziah was canny and tough. He wielded a tactical and political shrewdness that kept Assyria locked out.[2]

But now the king is dead. And with his death, the scales tilt—away from hope, toward instability and vulnerability and aloneness. Toward crisis.

Now what?

In that year, the prophet Isaiah goes to the temple. He's only a young man, just beginning, and I picture him confused, maybe dejected, maybe afraid, thinking, *Now what?* His massive shoulders bend down, arms drooped like so much dead weight. A huge sadness has reduced his eruptive energy, his bristling confidence, almost to timidity. He halts. He trudges. His big frame, the way it towers and hulks, seems a liability now. Just thicker bones to break, more weight to lug. There's more of him to hurt.

Maybe he's going to pray. You would, too. Crisis like this tumbles down on a nation. Planes hit the towers, and the need to pray comes on us like a fainting spell, overwhelming our best-laid defenses. And what might Isaiah's prayer be? *O Lord, help! God, we're in ruin. Our enemies swarm, swoop down.*

Do things, God. Fix things. Protect, heal, repair, restore. Rescue us!

But he never prays it. Because this is what comes next: "I saw the Lord seated on a throne, high and exalted, and the train of his robe filled the temple."

In the year King Uzziah died, Isaiah sees the real King. And he cries out, but the cry has nothing to do with national crisis or approaching enemies. His cry is wrenchingly personal: "Woe to me! I am ruined! For I am a man of unclean lips, and I live among a people of unclean lips, and my eyes have seen the King, the LORD Almighty."

The enemy is a scarecrow now. The national crisis is a gnat's bite. The big jostling sack of troubles Isaiah dragged into the temple shrinks in the mountainous presence of God to a tiny dust mote and blows away in the wind.

We often fail to grasp our greatest need in times of greatest need. When we are distressed, bewildered, threatened, shaken; in those moments when we want, more than anything, God to do something; when we wonder, more than ever, if there even is a God to do anything—in those moments of greatest need, our greatest need is simply to see the Lord. To see Him high and exalted. To see Him in His kingly majesty. To see Him in His perfect holiness. Nothing else can so quickly put our life into right perspective, scale it to true proportion.

Writer and pastor Eugene Peterson was asked, "What do you do when people come to you in distress and assume you can fix their problem?"

He said, "You have to go back a step and ask, 'Why am I a pastor? What is my primary responsibility to this congregation?'

"The most important thing a pastor does is stand in a pulpit every Sunday and say, 'Let us worship God.' If that ceases to be the primary thing I do in terms of my energy, my imagination, the way I structure my life, then I no longer function as a pastor.... I cannot fail to call the congregation to worship God, to listen to His Word, to offer themselves to God. Worship becomes a place where we have our lives redefined for us."[3]

That is our greatest need in times of greatest need: to have our lives redefined for us—ruined and remade—by a terrible, wonderful encounter with the King of glory. To see God as He really is.

And how *is* God, really? Who *is* this God, this sublime and exalted Being, this God beyond our knowing whom we long to know? If all His attributes were distilled down to one, crystallized in a single word, what would that word be?

The angels know.

The seraphim, you would think, must have a vast repertoire of songs, songs that evoke and celebrate the manifold beauty of the Lord—His love, His power, His goodness, His mercy. But of all the virtues they might worship, of all His excellencies they might extol, there is one thing they say, thrice repeated, back and forth, night and day, world without end: "Holy, holy, holy."[4]

God is holy.

❧ ❧ ❧

ISAIAH, THOUGH, CAN'T join the song, not yet. His life is being redefined for him. An encounter with God's holiness does that to us: It gives rise, not to song and dance, but to wild, harrowing terror. His holiness is heart-stopping, hair-raising. It scalds and rends and pierces. It elicits from our lips, our unclean lips, not "Wow!" but "Woe!"

When we see God, we also see ourselves. When we behold His holiness, we see in that instant our unholiness. His glory reveals our ruin, His purity our vanity, His light our shadows. God bursts forth in radiance, and we cry out for the rocks to fall on us. And so before joy comes sorrow. Before cleanness comes shame. Before we can ever rest in the holiness of God, first we must be undone by it.

The year I became a pastor, I saw the Lord. My first church was struggling, as churches are wont to do, with worship. And I was a greenhorn, all thumbs at this. Just before I arrived, the church had launched a "contemporary worship service." It was a makeshift, slapdash mess—a goulash of camp songs and slangy prayers and short-sleeved, open-neck attire. We muddled through. We scavenged for musicians, cobbled together songs. We were sharp-tongued with each other and thick-tongued with God. We got into exhausting squabbles about lyrical trivia, bruising rows over tempos and timing. The friction between us, like an old railway brake, often spat and crackled with sparks.

That first spring, I helped to organize a worship conference. We invited a worship team from a church in the next town over to lead us, because they were a bit further along in the direction we thought we were headed. We had no budget for this conference. Some people in the church thought it a bad idea. But I pressed on, out of stubbornness, naïveté, arrogance, and maybe, somewhere beneath all that, some holy folly, some genuine God-hunger. I fretted the details. I ran up a deficit. I mismanaged the schedule and manhandled the arrangements. Mostly, I let things sprawl where they fell.

But something changed in me that weekend. The second night, in the middle of one of the songs—a campy, clippity-clop number called "The Lord Reigns"—I started to tremble. It came on me slow, a prickling along my back, a shivering along my legs and arms. Something was loosing inside me, something I never knew was held back. Then the trembling broke out, my body shook, and I fell to my knees.

Suddenly, I was in the presence of God, and nothing else mattered. I didn't care what I looked like to others. I grasped, in an immediate, visceral way, what the Israelites must have felt when they saw the smoke and thunder and lightning on Mount Sinai, what the shepherds experienced in the fields as the night sky blazed with a glory of the heavenly host and the earth shook with their voices, what John knew when the angel whisked him into the midst of all creation kneeling before the throne of God. I knew what Isaiah knew. *Woe is me, for I am ruined, for I am a man of unclean lips and my eyes have seen the King, the Lord Almighty.* And at the same time, I knew I never wanted to be anywhere else.

GOD'S ESSENCE IS HOLINESS.[5]

But we have cheapened that word, warped it into carica-ture. A "holy" man, in our withered imaginations and shriveled vocabulary, is prudish and squeamish. He scolds and scowls, bristles with suspicion, his laughter full of scorn. His whole ethic is reduced to a litany of Thou Shalt Nots. Say "holy" on the street, maybe even in the church, and for most people it evokes images of Nathaniel Hawthorne's Puritans from *The Scarlet Letter*, a sour and wary folk bent on making everyone as miserable as they are. H. L. Mencken, the irreverent and very funny early-twentieth-century American journalist and histo-rian, remarked once that a Puritan was a man who feared that someone, somewhere, was having fun.

This is often the idea we import into the concept of holi-ness. And then we carry this idea over into our thinking when it comes to the holiness of God. The holy God becomes a cos-mic prig whose eyes range to and fro over the earth, seeking those who have messed up, that He might bludgeon them.

But this image is skewed as a bent nail.

The word *holiness* has two common meanings and a third

one buried under centuries of forgetfulness and dogma. Holiness, first, means *wholly other*. The holy God is totally separate from His creatures and His creation. His essential being is not bound up with anything or to anyone. He is utterly, completely free, independent. He needs not one thing for His life, His joy, His being God. God is God no matter what—whether we acknowledge Him or not, whether we worship Him or not, whether we obey Him or not. God's essence is not altered one iota by anything external to Him. His holiness is Wholly Otherness.

But there's a second meaning. Holiness is wholeness. It is perfect health. The holy God is without shadow or taint, without weakness or blemish. He embodies moral and spiritual perfection, and nothing in heaven or earth or under the earth can damage or diminish that. God is invulnerable to corruption or decay. He strives after nothing. He falls short in no way.

This second aspect of God's holiness, not the first, is what God calls His people to imitate. We cannot be wholly other, although we need in many ways to be set apart. Yet our earthbound lives will always be dependent—on God, on others, on creation. God wants it this way. The human desire to be wholly other is only the temptation of the garden recloaked. It is the dream of being complete unto ourselves, without finiteness, without boundaries—as gods. For us, this is always the way of death.

But God does want us to imitate the second aspect of His

holiness—to be whole. "Be holy, because I am holy."[6] The command and invitation here is to become, like God, healthy to the marrow, without the sour breath of envy, without the twisting and stunting in our limbs that greed or suspicion causes. Free. Unburdened by those many things that, promising to fulfill us, only betray us.

Christ said He was a doctor, going to the sick. When He healed people, His benediction was often, "Go, your faith has made you *whole*." His word and touch restored something that sickness or injury had ruined, some part of the individual that death had already blighted.

Christ's power and willingness to do this in the physical realm—to resculpt hands and feet ravaged by leprosy, to make pliant again eardrums that had become hard and brittle, to relight eyes smoked over with blindness, to reawaken a heart that had stopped and cooled—demonstrated that He also was willing and able to resurrect a soul dead to sin.

When some men brought their paralyzed friend to Jesus, tearing the house apart to get him there, Jesus declared, "Son, your sins are forgiven." This caused rumbling and murmuring among the teachers of law and the Pharisees: "Who can forgive sins but God alone?"

I imagine—though I'm only speculating—that it also caused bafflement and distress among the paralyzed man and his companions. They hadn't gone to all this trouble simply to get a pardon. They wanted a miracle. They wanted to see dead nerves spark to life, stiff flesh grow supple, wilted muscles stretch and tighten. They wanted to see the man dance a jig, toss a ball, do a handstand, pick up a stone.

Jesus does grant him this. "Get up, take your mat and walk," He says. But look at Jesus' motive for doing it: "*That you may know the Son of Man has authority on earth to forgive sins...I tell you, 'Get up, take your mat and go home.'"* Jesus performs the physical healing to establish His spiritual credentials. He does it to vouch for a greater authority that He possesses, a more staggering power He wields—the ability to forgive sins. To reform sin-ravaged hearts. To cleanse leprosy-numbed souls. To cure pride-blinded spirits. To cleanse folly-choked minds.[7]

To make us holy. To make us whole.

That is the second aspect of God's holiness, this amazing gift. And if we by faith venture into the wild and as-yet-undiscovered places of God, the gift of holiness will become our gift of wholeness, too. By His touch, we can trade our sorrows for His joy, our ashes for the oil of gladness.

THERE IS A THIRD ASPECT of holiness that we've largely forgotten about. I call it *wholly aliveness*. Wholly aliveness is that aspect of God's triune nature that most protects and liberates life in a community of believers. It is the canopy and taproot of our life together, guarding it, nourishing it. "If we walk in the light," John says, "as he is in the light, we have fellowship with one another."[8]

Human community always has some treachery lurking within it. We each have a hidden, broken part of ourselves—a self-loathing, a malcontent, a misery over being who we are—that we bleed into the community, sabotaging the intimacy we crave. Blame. Rivalry. Deceit. Contempt. Envy. Anger.

Holiness is our shield against this. Without holiness—the wholly aliveness of God's own life at work within us—all these things breed and spread, viruslike. The first human community, a man and a woman, bone of bone and flesh of flesh, was drenched through with holiness. They perfectly mimicked the God who exists as Father, Son, and Holy Spirit, in a relationship of love and self-giving. Adam and Eve were both naked and felt no shame. They were wholly alive, utterly content to be themselves and to be with each other. They each stood exposed, stripped to glorious nakedness, body and soul. Each could see the other through and through, every crease of skin, every ripple of thought. But there was no impulse to hide, to blame, to envy. There was no pride. In fact, there was a self-satisfaction that, rightfully embraced, is pride's opposite.

They were home. They were wholly alive.

It was good.

This, too, is holiness.

GOD'S HOLINESS BRAIDS together all three aspects—Wholly Otherness, Wholeness, Wholly Aliveness—in perfect completeness. Any one of these facets by itself is exquisite. Taken together, they comprise a dimension of God's character that is staggeringly beautiful and terrible. No wonder that when we see God high and lifted up—we who can no longer be naked without shame, we who have unclean lips and who live among a people of unclean lips—our first instinct is to recoil.

And it's Isaiah who shows us this.

Isaiah. Not Zacchaeus, the wily tax collector. Not Peter, the salt-tongued fisherman. Not Legion, the self-mutilating demoniac. Not David, the philandering king. Not Jonah, the reluctant prophet. It's Isaiah, a man who (at least in my image of him) towered with righteousness, from boyhood to decrepitude. In the presence of God's holiness, even Isaiah is undone.

Ironic that those most holy are least likely to see themselves that way.

This can't be faked, a response like this. It can't be prescribed like an exercise regimen or taught like a golf swing. But it can be lived out before us, in a way that leaves us stricken, aching, wanting more. Years ago, I was in Uganda, riding to church in the back of a rattling old truck, cheek by jowl with a crowd of others, black and white. The roads were mostly unpaved, and the vehicle threw up mounds of chalky red dust.

We were covered with it, and I wasn't very happy about that. We stopped at a small village to pick up yet more people, and many children, seeing the unusual sight of white people riding in the back of a pickup like field workers, gathered around, talking about us in their rapid-fire patois, giggling, pointing. I made some offhand remark. I don't remember what, other than that it was barbed, caustic.

A Ugandan man standing beside me looked straight at me. His clothes were threadbare from too many scrubbings, from the endless struggle to keep them clean. His skin was glazed with sweat and talcy with dust. "My brother," he said, "you should not say such things. You are a new creation in Christ. How can blessing and cursing come out of the same mouth? No unwholesome word should come out of your mouth, but only that which is useful for building others up according to their needs, that all who hear it would be edified."

He may as well have stuck bamboo shoots under my fingernails. He may as well shoved me naked through a gauntlet. I was undone. I was heading to church to preach that morning. This man would sit under my teaching, under my words.

A man of unclean lips.

What was hardest was the tone in which he said it. I wish he'd been sharp-edged and scolding, haughty in his disapproval—a right proud pharisee, holier than thou. But he wasn't like that at all. He said it with heartbreak. He said it pleadingly. He said it as one who had been burned in the fire and now lived to protect others, to warn them. He knew what it was to stand in the presence of a holy God and be undone.

Even in my shame, I longed to stand there, too.

But the good news is that God desires to share His holiness. He is not skittish with it, recoiling from us as we recoil at the sight of Him. He isn't stingy with it, hiding it from us like a child hoarding the last cookie. He is not defensive about it, wrapping Himself around it as though it's an orchid exposed to a winter storm, an infant beleaguered by wolves. His holiness is fierce and wild and hardy and takes care of itself. But God does want to compress His holiness into something hand-sized, like a brick of coal, and then press it, deep and searing, into us.

And so he does. With Isaiah, God sends one of His angels—one of the singing seraphs who, astoundingly, must pause his eternal paean to God's holiness to do this—and he brings a live altar coal. The angel enacts the severe mercy of God: He brands Isaiah lips. He burns him clean.

God is a consuming fire. Jesus did not come to bring peace—not first—but a fire and a sword, and how He wishes that fire were already kindled. The fire of God is this holiness, and it either destroys us or it cleanses us. T. S. Eliot, in his *Four Quartets,* says it so lyrically, we almost miss the utter starkness of our choice:

[Our] only hope, or else despair
lies in the choice of pyre of pyre—
to be redeemed from fire by fire...
We only live, only suspire
consumed by either fire or fire.[9]

Redeemed from fire by fire. In the face of God's holiness, we are either ruined or cleansed. Henry Miller began his book *The Tropic of Capricorn* with the mocking boast that he's never feared God, and if ever he saw God he'd spit in His face. Miller died in the early 1980s—he got to see God. This one thing is sure: He never spat in God's face. He had only two choices, if at that point he still had a choice: be consumed by God's fire, or be cleansed by it.

Isaiah chooses to be cleansed by fire.

In the movie *The Mission,* Robert De Niro plays Mendoza, the ruthless captain of a band of Spanish slave traders. He has grown rich on human plunder. Mendoza, in a fit of insane jealousy, kills his own brother and is crushed with guilt, plunged into moral and spiritual crisis. The missionary leader Gabriel, played by Jeremy Irons, seeks out Mendoza and convinces him that he must go to the people he once brutalized and enslaved and now serve them.

Mendoza cannot believe that his guilt can ever be removed. He joins the missionaries anyhow. They climb up steep cliffs, through gorges and ravines and dense forest, to where the tribe lives. In a vain attempt to atone for his guilt, Mendoza carries all the trappings of his former way of life. He stuffs a purse-net with his sword and armor and drags it behind him.

They finally arrive at the edge of the village. Mendoza is weak with exhaustion. The tribe people come out to greet them, but there is shocked silence when they see Mendoza, the man who has taken away their wives, their husbands, their sons, their daughters. No one moves. Then one man from the tribe approaches. He holds a knife in his hand, sharp and curved, gleaming cold.

Mendoza kneels, motionless. He's anchored down by his sack of guilt relics. He doesn't care anymore. There is no release, no atonement. He turns his neck upward, ready to receive what he deserves. The man stands over him, raises the knife and, with it, delivers his judgment. But instead of killing Mendoza, the tribesman severs the burden of his great sack of evil. The bundle falls away, tumbling over rock and root, and is swallowed up by the shadows of the jungle.

Gone.

In this moment, Mendoza's face changes. His whole body changes. The darkness has turned to light, the heaviness to levity, the grief to joy. He knelt a broken man and arises a healed one.

He fell down, ruined, and stands up whole...holy.[10]

That's what God does. The holiness of God at first consumes us, ruins us. But if we submit, it cuts the burden, burns the sin, and sets us free.

Be holy, because I am holy.

꒞ ꒞ ꒞

THERE'S ONLY ONE WAY to get there from here: worship. I've never met anyone who actually rests in God's holiness who has contemplated their way into it. You cannot get there with a fine parsing of Greek roots or a careful taxidermy of biblical images and theological themes. The experience is not like that. It's visceral, raw, scalding.

It only comes from seeing God.

We can't stage-manage that. But if there's one thing we can do to put ourselves in the place where this can happen, it's worship. A few summers ago, for several weeks, there was a buzz about town. On a Saturday night in August, the skies would blaze with a cataract of meteorites, a downpour of shimmering, burning rock. The weather was going to be perfect—clear and moonless, with a coolness that sharpened visibility. And we were in a corner of the hemisphere that gave us front-row seats. The best time to see it was actually early Sunday morning at 2 A.M. I set my alarm for 1:55 and told my son I'd wake him, and we would stand in our bathrobes on the deck and behold the wonders of the heavenly hosts.

I never woke up. I had set the alarm for P.M., not A.M. I sailed right on through to morning.

Church was galling that Sunday. Person after person came up to me, asking, "Did you see it?"

"No."

"You missed it? Oh, you really missed something. I wouldn't have missed that for anything. It was like watching a shoot-out in *Star Wars*. I can't believe you missed it...."

On and on, person after person.

The heavens don't always light up like that. But when they do, only those who are awake and standing beneath the heavens get to see it.

Likewise, God doesn't always reveal Himself high and lifted up, His glory filling the temple. Most Sundays, we catch at best a grainy outline, like those putative photos of Bigfoot or Nessie. Most trips to the temple only leave us with a fleeting glimpse of His back side, a shadow of movement at the corner of our eye. But then there are other times when God surprises us, dazzles us, terrifies us, and heals us. We are undone, and we are remade.

He shows us His holiness.

But only those awake and watching get to see it.

Writer Anne Lamott tells of a moment like that:

> One of our newest members, a man named Ken Nelson, is dying of AIDS, disintegrating before our very eyes. He came in a year ago with a Jewish woman who comes every week to be with us, although she does not believe in Jesus. Shortly after the man with AIDS started coming, his partner died of the disease. A few

weeks later Ken told us that right after Brandon died, Jesus had slid into the hole in his heart that Brandon's loss left, and has been there ever since. Ken has a totally lopsided face, ravaged and emaciated, but when he smiles he is radiant.... He says that he would gladly pay any price for what he has now, which is Jesus, and us.

Lamott goes on to tell about a woman in her church, Ranola, who "is large and black and devout as can be," but who has been a "little standoffish toward Ken." Ranola views Ken with suspicion, fear, a bit of disgust. "I think she and a few other women at church are, on the most visceral level, a little afraid of catching the disease."

But Kenny has come to church almost every week for the last year and won almost everyone over. He finally missed a couple of Sundays when he got too weak, and then a month ago he was back, weighing almost no pounds, his face even more lopsided, as if he'd had a stroke. Still, during the prayers of the people, he talked joyously of his life and decline, of grace and redemption, of how happy and safe he feels these days.

And then the congregation began to sing. Kenny was too weak to stand, so he sang sitting down, the hymnal open on his lap because he lacked strength to hold it.

> And then when it came time for the second hymn, the fellowship hymn, we were to sing "His Eye Is on the Sparrow." The pianist was playing and the whole congregation had risen—only Ken remained seated, holding the hymnal in his lap—and we began to sing, "Why should I feel discouraged? Why do the shadows fall?" And Ranola watched Ken rather skeptically for a moment, and then her face began to melt and contort like his, and she went to his side and bent down to lift him up—lifted up this white rag doll, this scarecrow. She held him next to her, draped over her like a child while they sang. And it pierced me.
>
> I can't imagine anything but music that could have brought about this alchemy.[11]

I can't imagine anything but worship—glimpsing God's holiness in a way that ruins us and heals us—that could do this.

THE APOSTLE JOHN, near the end of his life, was caught up into worship, and he saw what Isaiah had nearly eight hundred years before.

> There before me was a throne in heaven with someone sitting on it. And the one who sat there had the appearance of jasper and carnelian.... In the center, around the throne, were four living creatures, and they were covered with eyes, in front and in back.... Each of the four living creatures had six wings and was covered with eyes all around, even under his wings. Day and night they never stop saying: "Holy, holy, holy is the Lord God Almighty, who was, and is, and is to come."
>
> Then I looked and heard the voice of many angels, numbering thousands upon thousands, and ten thousand times ten thousand. They encircled the throne and the living creatures and the elders. In a loud voice they sang: "Worthy is the Lamb, who was slain, to receive power and wealth and wisdom and strength and honor and glory and praise!"
>
> Then I heard every creature in heaven and

on earth and under the earth and on the sea, and all that is in them, singing: "To him who sits on the throne and to the Lamb be praise and honor and glory and power, for ever and ever!"[12]

John's vision mirrors and echoes Isaiah's. The seraphim, all these centuries later, still sing their song of God's holiness, never tiring.

But two things are different. Eight hundred years before, only the angels sang. Heaven's music was performed by an elite company, a chamber choir of angels. But now, all heaven and earth join the song. It is no longer an aria for a few, but a chorus of all creation.

The second difference is more significant. In Isaiah's vision, the seraphim around God's throne use two of their wings to cover their eyes. Even though they are holy, they cannot behold the perfection of God's holiness. It is too much even for them to look upon.

But in John's vision, the creatures who surround God's throne are "covered with eyes, in front and in back." Each has six wings and is "covered with eyes all around, even under his wings." They are *all* eyes. They can do no other than look full upon the Lord high and lifted up.

Why? What has changed in those eight hundred years? Just this: "Then I saw a Lamb, looking as if it had been slain, standing in the center of the throne."[13]

"Look, the Lamb of God," John the Baptist once declared, "who takes away the sin of the world!"[14]

The difference is Jesus, the Lamb of God, who takes away the sins of anyone, of everyone, of all who call on His name. Me, a man of unclean lips. You. Because of Jesus, what once was forbidden for angels to look upon now all eyes can see, and the song that once mighty prophets dared not sing now all creation can join.

Holy, holy, holy is the Lord God Almighty.

Part III

SEARCH
THESE WOODS

*How God's Majestic Nature Is
Made Manifest in the World*

༈ ༈ ༈ ༈ ༈ ༈ ༈ ༈ ༈ ༈

Chapter Nine

WHERE THE STONES SING

God's Creativity

Most Protestant churches are graveyards for the imagination. They are about the last place on earth you expect to find good art. Sentimental kitsch, yes. Schmaltzy propaganda, yes. But good art, no. There is nothing that startles or subdues, haunts or grips; nothing that awakens an instinct to coil tight and leery around your terrible secrets, or to drop all your guards, fling wide your arms, and spill everything. I have never *in a church* seen a rendering of Eden that made me want to visit the place, or of a serpent who could seduce me into the forbidden. I have never seen there a depiction of the Last Supper that pierced me with longing and sorrow. I have, for that matter, never seen a single portrait of Jesus that made me want to lose my inhibitions and lean my head against His chest.

I have never seen the Holy Wild, stark, threatening, enticing.

There is, I know, a long history behind all this, some of it dreary and bewildering, some of it vivid and instructive. But I am not here to recite that history, partly because I know it only in bits and pieces, but mostly because I want to do something else.

I want to rediscover the God who makes things. I want to renew our worship of the God boundless and whimsical in creativity, who sculpts and weaves, paints and cobbles, carves and stipples with consummate control yet giddy abandon. God sometimes seems like Jackson Pollock, dribbling and smearing color in loops and daubs across a vast canvas. Sometimes like Georgia O'Keeffe, everything held close to the eye, layered with ethereal shades, filled with an otherworldly glow. Sometimes like a Dutch master, observing the minutest detail with meticulous care, choosing dimension and perspective and hue with a watchmaker's precision, rendering it all in serene simplicity, luminous and solid as a vase in sunlight.

I walked the beach today. You can't do this with your senses even half open and not leave wonder-struck. So much color, movement, music, shape, fragrance. The extravagance. Just look at all the shells, their fluted edges or spiny backs, their whorls and cones and ribs and fantails, their pearly iridescent insides. You really can, in the bigger shells—the ones that spiral in on themselves with openings big as a bass mouth—hear the sea as far away as the desert or the prairies, if you press your ear in close. In some of them, hermit crabs move in after the meaty slithery creatures who first bore these brittle shells move out, and this is a wonder, too: these skittish creatures, their proportionally enormous foreclaws thick as Popeye's arms, tucked up into the shell's inner chambers like skulking thieves planning their heist.

Or just look at the seaweed: ocher-colored sheets, ragged like parchment, stippled across their surface as though with Braille; long, eel-like tubes, tapering ropelike at one end and swelling into bulbous heads at the other; ribbony, slippery strips, crepe-paper thin; light green swaths of filigree, hollow throughout; dark green slabs, thick and rough-skinned as cow tongues; intricate root bundles, convoluted as brain tissue. Mounds and skeins and nests of it everywhere. When I come here with my children, we have seaweed festivals. We set up a seaweed salon, where you can have your hair done in any number of styles and colors of seaweed. We have a seaweed café, where you can get pastas and soups and desserts and appetizers, all concocted from things we pick up on the rocks, served in clamshells or on flat pieces of driftwood. And we go on a snake-hunting expedition, battling, with our bare hands, thirty-foot lengths of kelp, stomping on their ballooning heads so that they split and splat, gushing briny water.

You couldn't name it all in a lifetime. You would have to plunder dictionaries in twelve languages to describe adequately one square foot of it. All this God makes for the sheer joy of making things, most of it for His eyes only, and then goes off and makes something else.

ONE OF THE STRONGEST evidences that we are not resting much in God or risking much for God is the lowly state of the arts among Christians. The Spirit brooded over the formless void and conjured living things, intricate and exotic things, from a poem. If that same Spirit, who raised Jesus from the dead, also lives in you and me, why aren't we more creative? Lovers of God should, by osmosis, know an irrepressible urge to be poets, artists, artisans. We should make things and make them well. Canadian writer Michael St. George was asked when he first became a poet. He thought a moment, then said, "When did most of us stop being poets? Kids are just natural artists—they sing, dance, make up poems.... Everyone is basically creative."[1]

When did most of us stop being poets? When did you stop being a poet or a painter or a sculptor or a singer?

Books about God often talk about God as Creator—the maker of heaven and earth—but not as Artist—the maker of dragonflies and pussy willows. We extol His power in creation, but ignore His extravagant, exuberant *creativity,* His sheer inventiveness and playfulness. There might be a lingering gnosticism in all this, a squeamishness about implicating God too deeply in the gritty details of creation, as though it robs Him of grandeur if He's too hands-on, too spattered with paint or up to His elbows in wet clay. Yet as artists from Fyodor Dostoyevsky to Dorothy Sayers to Madeleine L'Engle have remarked, the human desire—even need—to create simply mirrors the God in whose image we are made, by whose breath we are filled. John says we love because God first loved us. That phrase, tweaked a little, could be turned into a foundational formula for explaining anything worthwhile we do: We love mercy because He first loved mercy; we do justly because He first did justly.

We make poems because He first made poems.

When did you stop being a poet?

One thing that stifles the artistic impulse in us is we try too hard. We also try too little. We neither submit to the discipline required, nor give in to the impulse to let go. We don't press in far enough, and we don't relinquish fully enough.

But let's talk about trying too hard. Christians are generally driven by a desire to edify. We want what we do to have a meaning, a moral, a message. So the things we put our hands to usually get shaped in that mold and pressed into that service: Our poems teach, our paintings proclaim, our stories make points. To a certain extent, this is good. But just walking from the front door to the sidewalk, I get the impression that God isn't overburdened with the same impulse. He just likes making things, in myriad shape and color, no particular rhyme or reason. Flowers. Bugs. Birds. Stones. God, like an eccentric inventor who creates for the sheer quirky joy of it, just keeps flinging out innovations and variations, and we run behind like harried assistants, trying to keep inventories.

Hebrews describes Jesus as the author and perfecter of our faith. But the story of my faith is a puzzling, disheveled thing so far. As an author, I'd give it more drama, more structure, more instructional ballast. I'd work in a twist of intrigue here, a fillip of high adventure there. And I would be more didactic, sharper and cleaner in my application of moral truth.

The actual story of my faith has been disjointed and fragmented, a ragbag of half-done and ill-shaped themes, with characters who drop in and out and a few who hang on too long, with a plot that fizzles in one direction, careens off wildly in another. Jesus is to blame. He's the author of this. I'm beginning to think His literary conventions are, well, a tad eccentric, like James Joyce's.

God doesn't seem to try too hard. He just makes things, most of which mean no more and no less than themselves.

Let me speak as a writer. Writing is making something almost from nothing. It's conjuring people, places, situations out of air that, if not completely thin, is rarefied as Everest's.

But that makes it sound like magic. Most of my writing experience has not been magical. It's been long seasons of plowing and trudging, with the odd spring or harvest festival to break up the drudgery. It's been a waddle across a muddy tidal flat, occasionally with a surprising thermal updraft that catches you under the wing and carries you airborne for a short, awkward burst.

I've never gotten used to it, writing, though I do it most days, just like I was told. Every day the blank page—or computer screen, in my case—seems only to reflect back my own blankness. Or, if it's partially filled, it taunts me with its unfinishedness, like those houses people start and then, black and tattery with tar paper and hollow inside, abandon partway through, a permanent monument to their failure, their bankruptcy, their divorce. It doesn't matter, it turns out, that I'm published, that people have paid me good money for my writing. Every morning, I feel like a novice, sometimes like a fraud, most times like a has-been trying to make the stone spark fire again, to get the thick, cold sap flowing, to get the muse to at least blink, move her lips, show some sign of life. Writer's block? It's an intimate companion, so close I'd feel almost forsaken if ever it left me.

The writing is never so bad as when I'm straining at it. I'm like the old quarry prisoner, spending my days breaking big rocks into little ones. And then I get panicky and start pushing, hitting too hard. All this does is make me sore faster. And usually it makes fewer rocks.

Don't misunderstand, writing takes enormous discipline. It takes a willingness to show up each day and hit the rock, steady, methodical, regimented, again and again and again. But part of the discipline is waiting. It is dwelling, quiet and patient, in the presence of the creative God. He never runs out of fresh ideas, new angles, dazzling variations on old themes, innovative recycling of used material. He makes masterpieces out of scavenged things and waste things—gardens from rotted orange rinds and sodden coffee grounds, jewels from lumps of coal He long ago tucked down deep into a crack in the earth and left to bake. He can take any bone shard or scruff of fur or bit of gristle and spin from it a whole new creation.

I have a musical friend who is so gifted that my own musicianship—always a slapdash fumbling kind of thing—improves from just spending time with him. His musical nimbleness limbers me up. His joy in the way a deft hand or supple voice can embellish a single note, give it a wild array of textures—making a simple A-note light and airy one moment, brusque and earthy the next, solid and matter-of-fact the next—stirs a kindred joy in me. His passion and skillfulness spill over, and I sop up the spill.

And so it is with God. Our creativity, at least in part, comes from resting in His creativity until it seeps in. It springs from prayer. Not the busy chatty prayer we often do, but the other kind: prayer as emptiness, prayer as silence, prayer as stillness. Prayer as the absence of wanting and asking. Not the clamoring man waking his neighbor, desperate for bread, but the suckled child curled up, satisfied in the mother's arms.

Sometimes I just sit there. I don't speak or ask or think. I watch, devoid of analysis. No attempt to split any atom or crack any code or discern any pattern or espy any meaning. No sifting or sorting or figuring out. I quiet the lust of the writer to filch beauty or terror from every experience, to pilfer from dazzling wonders mere illustrations, to plagiarize creation. I just sit and look.

I look at the holographic strangeness of water, the shifting surface, reflecting, revealing, hiding, disclosing. One minute, water will lie still and everything above it—faces, sky, mountains, trees—will imprint on its silvery surface an image as clean as a photograph. The next, the light will shift, a breeze will stir, and everything above and beneath the surface splinters and disappears. Then another shift of light, a dead calm, and the surface melts away to unveil the water's buried secrets. Or I look at the infinite variety of wood and stone, and all the things you can make from a single piece of ash—a bow, a nightstand, a walking stick, a window frame, a door.

I let these things be, and I simply dwell in their presence. Where there is music or poetry or artistry in these things, I receive it without comment or lament, without the impulse to possess it or explain it. There is nothing mystical about this. This is not a slipping toward pantheism, where every rock bluff or grass tuft brims with divinity. This is simply an act of reverence for the God who makes things, and respect for all that He makes.

And then sometimes, God shows up and makes the stones sing. He sidles up alongside, like an artist whose work you are admiring in a museum slipping in just behind your right shoulder and telling you one small, illuminating story about what he was thinking when he made the thing you're looking at. It's not what I bargain for, this moment when God touches and speaks anew the thing He's made. Well, it is, but I've learned that there's no use making demands here. It just happens, or it doesn't. But when it does, it is both wonderful and ordinary, a mystery suspiciously familiar.

GOD'S CREATIVITY IS, in one sense, the most obvious thing about Him. He grandstands it, parades His crafts and wares and potions, brash and gaudy as a gypsy's wagon. But in another sense, God's creativity is hidden. He's elusive with it, playful, coy. Much of what He makes He tucks away, in microscopic minuteness or cosmic immensity, deep beneath us or far above us. He saves His most intricate work for the insides and undersides of things. I read recently that the sound whales make blowing through their airholes, that deep foghornish bellow, actually appears to be a music, a symphony of deep calling to deep.

We have, by an industry and ingenuity that is itself God-given, managed somehow to name most of these things, to sort them into complex patterns and categories, to arrange them in neat taxonomic grids, to trace the tangled threads that connect anteaters to bears, salamanders to crocodiles. But that's our task, our problem. "It is the glory of God to conceal a matter; to search out a matter is the glory of kings."[2] The cosmos is God's playground, His vast park for playing hide-and-seek.

Science has become of late an ideological theater of war, where a pitched battle between creationists and evolutionists rages. This is maybe necessary, perhaps healthy, but in some profound and heartrending ways it misses the point entirely. The earth, the heavens, the seas—all is a gallery of wonders, a giant field strewn with treasure, some tossed there at random, others secreted away with great cunning.

Years ago, when our children were small, a couple from the church would invite us, along with several other families, every year for an Easter party. They had a large yard in a rural area—a place where you could set a big pit fire right on your own front lawn and no one would look askance—and on the Saturday between Good Friday and Easter Sunday they'd host a hot dog and marshmallow roast. On their property was a strip of forested area with thick-trunked cedars, with their ragged bark and drooping boughs; arrow-straight fir trees; spindly poplars; one or two burled and wizened garry oaks; and a few twisted arbutus, their barkless limbs smooth-skinned as Jacob, ruddy as Esau.

Amidst the trees was a crosshatch of well-worn trails. Between the hot dogs and the marshmallows, the children were set loose on these forest trails. Hidden in the forest was probably ten pounds of candy. Some of it was in plain sight—chocolate eggs wrapped in brilliant foil, perched atop a rotting stump at the trail's head, or scattered along the pathway's mossy curb. The older children were told to leave these for the younger ones. Other candy took a bit of scouting for—packets of gumdrops nestled into the pocket formed where tree roots join tree trunk. But other candy—for the older kids—required the cleverness of a sleuth, the guile of a bounty hunter, the persistence of a Mountie. There were chocolates embedded in the holes in the bark left by woodpeckers. There was silvery-papered nougat lying camouflaged among cinque-foil, and dark-wrapped toffee squirreled away in root crevices. At first, the children struck out in a kind of militant panic, afraid they'd be left empty-handed. But the host couple had overstocked those woods, and soon the children realized that each would get a sizable sackful, and so they could slow down, enjoy the hunt. There was always enough for all.

I loved watching them run, scramble, clamber, discover. The truth is, I ached to join them. The pleasure of treasure hunting is a quirk of instinct. God wired us for this, that the simple act of searching out hidden things—candy, the Loch Ness monster, microbes on Mars, DNA patterns, a cure for migraines, your family tree, your birth parents—would stir our deepest blood; that a melee of young children on a candy grab would rouse my desire to risk, to dare, to conquer. There was a time a few years back when people used to talk about their inner child, a fearful, hopeful, fragile part of themselves that got wounded or neglected and never grew up. My inner child is more like a Little Rascal or Young Indiana Jones: It never got enough of wildfaring adventure and end-of-the-world expeditions, and now sits restless and listless most days, though it is quickly awakened by the mere sight of children beachcombing or kite-flying or stuffing their pockets with foil-covered candy.

Or maybe this is no child at all, but is the *king* in me. *It is the glory of God to conceal a matter, the glory of kings to search it out.*

And not only that—not only is God up to tricks and pranks with creation, doing sleight of hand with it, conjuring wonders from mud, pulling rabbits and elephants and galaxies from dust motes, seeds, thin air, tugging out an endless string of surprises from His sleeve—but He Himself plays hide-and-seek with us. "Truly," Isaiah says, "you are a God who hides himself."[3]

Jesus did this, played this game of hide-and-seek. The risen Christ, in one instance, walked a long road to Emmaus with two of His disciples. Not until He sat down with them, broke bread, and gave thanks—peeking out from behind this familiar gesture, nudging them with memories still fresh—did they recognize Him. And right then, He vanished, magician-like.

He did things like that more than once. Jesus could be a chameleon, a master of disguises. He walked on water, and His followers thought Him a ghost. He surprised Mary in front of His tomb, and she mistook Him for the gardener. At the end of the age, He'll tell us, "I came to you hungry, naked, I was in prison. I was wearing disguises." There are, I know, a number of explanations for why He hid, why He disguised Himself, why those closest to Him at times struggled to recognize Him. We ascribe it to the befuddlement of the disciples, their spiritual grogginess, their grief-skewed eyes, their lingering superstitions, their rigid dogmatisms. As well, or otherwise, we infer some supposed dramatic alterations in Jesus' physical appearance after His resurrection. If nothing else, it's part of the mystery of incarnation, God among us.

But I wonder if Jesus wasn't at times just playing. Back when I did youth ministry, one of the youth's favorite activities was a scavenger hunt with a twist. We recruited six or ten people who were well-known among the young people—the pastor, the youth pastor, two or three parents, a couple of older youth, the church custodian—and sent them down to the mall disguised. One man dressed up as a dowdy old woman, hunched and rumpled, his wigged hair held down by a bright floral babushka. One woman dressed as a man, with a thick, black beard and grease-stained workman's clothes.

One guy posed as a middle-aged businessman, paunchy and weary, toting an attaché case. We then took the youth to the mall, gave them a list of the people they were to look for, told them plainly that these people were disguised, and then set them loose. They had one hour to find all the fugitives and have them initial the scavenger list.

Not once did anyone uncover the entire contingent. Some could find no more than two or three. One of the most stunning moments was when a girl failed to recognize her own father, even though she walked past him three times and once even sat on a bench next to him. He asked her for the time and, oblivious, she gave it to him, got up, and walked away.

I'm sure Jesus had other, deeper, more theologically responsible reasons for His veiled appearances. But God has repeatedly shown His playfulness, His whimsy, His prankish sense of humor. Who else would have thought up an anteater except a great cosmic comic? And so I venture that God, notwithstanding the deep responsible theological reasons, was also just having fun.

Truly You are a God who hides Himself.

Seldom do we play, and rare is our wonder, and I wonder how much of God we're missing.

❧ ❧ ❧

JOB. IT'S A SMALL IRONY, available only to those who speak English, that the name of the man who suffered most hideously and the name of the work we do to survive are identically spelled. We do our jobs Job-like, seeking hopelessly to find meaning in them, to wrench from the drudgery and agony some glimmer of higher purpose, some sense of *why*. I have had many, many people sit in my study and describe their workaday world to me. The round and round and round repetition of menial tasks. The weariness deep as a bone disease. The glowering, thankless taskmasters who rule over them. The squabbling and gossiping and nitpicking of the staff. The cliques and battle lines and pecking orders. The pathetic pay. The toll on their families. The loss of joy. The tragic sense that this job consumes them, that it long ago devoured their youth and dreams and left behind only a thickening residue of sadness and bitterness.

Job. Job. It's the same word. And always, when faced again with someone's litany of their hardscrabble existence, I'm tempted to turn into one of Job's comforters, uttering pious-sounding nonsense, the lullaby of cheap consolation, the scolding of smug rebuke. To tell the man writhing on the dung pile, scraping his wounds with potsherds, that this must be his fault somehow. To explain to the woman who's had such little time lately for her children it's like the house collapsed on them that she needs to be more disciplined.

God doesn't do this. God meets Job's pain and his comforter's arrogance with a whirlwind tour of His art gallery, His inventor's lab, His manufacturer's plant.

> *"Look at the land beast, Behemoth.*
> *I created him as well as you.*
> *Grazing on grass, docile as a cow—*
> *Just look at the strength of his back,*
> *the powerful muscles of his belly.*
> *His tail sways like a cedar in the wind;*
> *his huge legs are like beech trees.*
> *His skeleton is made of steel,*
> *every bone in his body hard as steel.*
> *Most magnificent of all my creatures,*
> *but I still lead him around like a lamb!*
> *The grass-covered hills serve him meals,*
> *while field mice frolic in his shadow.*
> *He takes afternoon naps under shade trees,*
> *cools himself in the reedy swamps,*
> *Lazily cool in the leafy shadows*
> *as the breeze moves through the willows.*
> *And when the river rages he doesn't budge,*
> *stolid and unperturbed even when the Jordan goes wild.*
> *But you'd never want him for a pet—*
> *you'd never be able to housebreak him!"*[4]

And it's enough to convince Job:

> *"I'm speechless, in awe—words fail me.*
> *I should never have opened my mouth!*
> *I've talked too much, way too much.*
> *I'm ready to shut up and listen....*
> *You asked, 'Who is this muddying the water,*
> *ignorantly confusing the issue,*
> *second-guessing my purposes?'*
> *I admit it. I was the one.*
> *I babbled on about things far beyond me....*
> *I admit I once lived by rumors of you;*
> *now I have it all firsthand—from my own eyes and ears!*
> *I'm sorry—forgive me. I'll never do that again, I promise!*
> *I'll never again live on crusts of hearsay,*
> *crumbs of rumor."*[5]

I know that the standard way to understand this is to read God's portion as a divine taunt: *You don't understand the basics of botany and biology and zoology, you can't even grasp the nature of things all around you, you can't figure out the natural— so how dare you presume to understand the supernatural? You don't even get how egrets give birth. So why do you think you can comprehend My ways?*

But I'm going to miss the point entirely—and intention- ally. Maybe God's not taunting or scolding Job at all, or at least not just this. Instead, or perhaps as well, God is wooing him. He's dazzling him. He's answering his misery and agony and boredom with a call to fresh wonder, trying to make Job child-like again. He's saying, in effect, *Look, Job! Look at what I've made! You have been sitting on this dung pile so long, with this pain in your heart and in your flesh so long, with these boring windbags haranguing you for so long, that you've grown blind to beauty. Everyone's trying to fix you, Job, fix your problem. Not Me. I'm going to wow you. I'm going to put fire back in your belly.*

I have actually started doing this. When people come to me dreary, weary, worn out, cynical, people whose chronic suffering or treadmill life has narrowed their world down to the aches in their joints, the bills piling up, the stone on their back, I don't try to solve the problem much anymore. I try to get them to notice something else, something right in front of them which they haven't seen or heard or touched or smelled in a long, long time. The sound of water moving across stone. The shape of clouds. The pattern grass makes on the back of your legs when you've sat on it for a while, like hieroglyphs, or like the scrabble of bird claw in soft clay. The amazing changes, the withering and stiffening and whitening and deepening, that happen in people as they grow old.

I try to help them be childlike again.

᠀ ᠀ ᠀

I AM A DIVER. I find diving both familiar and freakish, the thing I was born for, the thing I'll never get used to. It's a wonder and a dread: the icy murky depths, vastly silent; the threat always, at least in my mind, of some hideous leviathan, huge and horned and scaly, unwieldy in shape but agile in motion, stalking me; the hypnotic swaying of underworld forests; the skittishness of fish and crab. But the beauty is transfixing and keeps enticing me under. The sight of a single giant anemone in full bloom, gaudy as a Harlequin, is breathtaking. And to spy an octopus in his den, his tentacles curled up under him like a nest and his sleepless lidless eye staring you down, is ecstasy.

When I took my diving lessons, the instructor went around the room of students and asked each of us why we were there. One man said it was because he always wanted to dive, and now he had a little time on his hands. Another said his friends all were divers, and he envied them and was tired of always being the guy left up at the surface, manning the boat.

When my turn came, I said that I was going through a midlife crisis and this was cheaper than a Corvette. That sparked predictable laughter. But then I shared the real reason: that I had lived above and on the water, and even in it, all my life, but I had never visited its depths. I had spent forty-two years skimming surfaces, merely wading, dabbling. Twenty feet under was as mysterious and dangerous to me as outer space. Fifty or sixty feet seemed another galaxy. It was starting to trouble me, that I had lived this long, had traveled far above the water and far out on it but had never gone deep beneath it. An entire other world stood close as the next corner, yet was as remote as Antarctica, as hidden as the earth's core. I wanted to enter it. I wanted to immerse myself in it.

And there was one other reason, but I only thought of it later: I don't play enough, and I don't rest enough. I am closing in on fifty, and my life has become narrowed down to deadlines and appointments and conferences and business lunches, chores and duties and tasks and projects. It had been ages since I had last cartwheeled through a meadow or danced to an old seventies song or slept in and not felt guilty or slightly stained, as though nursing a hangover.

It had been ages since I'd immersed myself in anything and just sat still and waited.

And sometimes God hides right there, waiting with me for the stones to sing.

Chapter Ten

A HAVEN FOR FOOLS

God's Wisdom

S everal summers past, the *Vancouver Sun* published excerpts of some gaffes from real-life courtroom cross-examinations:

- "Now doctor, isn't it true that when a person dies in his sleep, he doesn't know about it until the next morning?"
- "The youngest son, the twenty-year-old, how old is he?"
- "Were you present when your picture was taken?"

And here are some real responses to lawyers' questions:

Q: "Is your appearance here this morning pursuant to a deposition notice which I sent to your attorney?"

A: "No, this is how I dress when I go to work."

Q: "All your responses must be oral, okay? What school did you go to?"

A: "Oral."

And my favorite:

Q: "Doctor, before you performed the autopsy, did you check for a pulse?"

A: "No."

Q: "Did you check for blood pressure?"

A: "No."

Q: "Did you check for breathing?"

A: "No."

Q: "So then, is it possible that the patient was alive when you began the autopsy?"

A: "No."

Q: "How can you be so sure, doctor?"

A: "Because his brain was sitting on my desk in a jar."

Q: "But could the patient have still been alive nevertheless?"

A: "It is possible that he could have been alive and practicing law somewhere."[1]

God gave us laughter, I think, as a balm to wash the wounds of our own blunders, as a splint to mend the bones we break in our rashness or vanity. But laughter or no, I am amazed at times by my own folly.

And I'm not just talking about how little I know. That in itself is staggering. My children can ask me the simplest questions, questions about things I've spent my whole life observing, and I am stumped.

"Dad, how come there's different kinds of clouds?" Um, uh, wind and, um, temperature and the amount of moisture in the air and dust particles and...I don't know.

"Daddy, how does a television work?" Well, see, there's these, you know, electric sort of thingies that, um, you can store information in and transfer them to little doohickeys that sort them and...I'm not sure.

"Dad, why did Grampa have to die?"

The simplest things can throw me. But I'm not talking about my silly mistakes or my plumb ignorance. I'm talking about my folly, my amazing lack of wisdom. Wisdom is more than knowing things; it's knowing what to do with the things you know. It's the art of living well, living so that you and all around you benefit. That's wisdom.

And at times I am shockingly deficient in it. I *know* that a cup of coffee at eight o'clock at night will keep me up until three in the morning, and my tossing in the bed will drive my wife to thoughts of torture and murder. I drink it anyhow. I *know* that a word of kindness at a crucial moment will bring peace, healing, and reconciliation; it will calm the rage, quell the storm. I speak a word of harshness anyhow. I *know* what the Lord requires of me—to do justly, love mercy, and walk humbly with Him. I still sometimes choose otherwise.

Wisdom—at least human wisdom—is the art of living well. By that measure, some of the smartest people in the world are among the stupidest. Journalist and historian Paul Johnson documented this in his book *Intellectuals,* a collection of mini-biographies of leading thinkers of the last two hundred years, men and women whose ideas shaped whole cultures, began revolutions, and toppled civilizations. Karl Marx, Jean-Jacques Rousseau, Bertrand Russell, Henrik Ibsen, Lillian Hellman, others. Johnson shows in every instance that these men and women possessed massive intellects but puny souls. They lacked wisdom. They were cruel, shallow, heartless, selfish. They loved humanity but hated people.[2]

I think of some of the histories of the Vietnam War—David Halberstam's *The Best and the Brightest,* Barbara Tuchman's *The March of Folly,* Neil Sheehan's *A Bright Shining Lie.* Each leads to one overriding conclusion: The smartest people in the world are capable of making—no, *prone* to make—the stupidest choices. Knowledge is no guarantee of wisdom.

The apostle Paul opens his letter to the Romans by describing people like that. They're the people against whom God reveals His wrath. Paul puts it this way:

> For although *they knew God,* they neither glo-
> rified him as God nor gave thanks to him, but
> their thinking became futile and their foolish
> hearts were darkened. *Although they claimed to
> be wise,* they became fools.[3]

For although they knew God, although they claimed to be wise, they became fools.

Christians are hardly immune to this. Take Peter, for example. One minute he's declaring that Jesus is the Messiah, and the next minute, Peter is telling Jesus what He can and can't do, provoking this harsh rebuke from Jesus: "Get behind me, Satan!... You do not have in mind the things of God, but the things of men."[4]

Our mouths—and hearts—mix wisdom and folly freely. Like Peter, we weave together insight and myopia, shrewdness and obtuseness. We're a patchwork of silk and rags, a braid of straw and hemp.

* * *

PAUL DESCRIBES IN HIS LETTER to the Romans a world awash in folly. But he ends the letter with this dedication and benediction: "*To the only wise* God be glory forever through Jesus Christ! Amen."[5]

To the only wise God. God is not just the only one who is

truly wise, but He is *only wise*. There is no shade of folly in Him. Wisdom saturates everything He is and everything He does.

Which begs the question, *Really?*

In 1999, during a presidential debate, George W. Bush was asked, "Who is your favorite political philosopher?"

"Jesus Christ," he answered.

This stunned the audience, and afterward the press had a field day, a carnival of mockery. Douglas Groothuis, in an article in *Books & Culture,* citing that event, notes that in most authoritative encyclopedias of philosophy, Jesus is not listed in the roster of history's great thinkers. Buddha makes the cut. But not Jesus.[6] The irony of this is glaring. The very word *philosopher* means "lover of wisdom." Scripture describes Jesus as "the wisdom of God."[7] Just as God as Father is meant to be the touchstone of all earthly fathers, just as Christ as husband is meant to be our template for all human marriages, so God as the "only wise" One is meant to be the epitome of all philosophers. God in Christ is the Original Thinker.

Apparently, this slipped the notice of the gatekeepers.

It may have slipped more than their notice. The wisdom of God is one of those attributes that we simultaneously have oceans of evidence for and mountains of evidence against. As I write this, Severe Acute Respiratory Syndrome (SARS) is wreaking havoc in various cities in China and in Toronto, Canada. In Beijing, the mayor was fired for failing to deal swiftly and decisively with the outbreak, as if the plague were *his* fault. In

Toronto, the mayor is ranting at the World Health Organization for their mismanagement of the situation. Accusations are flying back and forth that health professionals—doctors, nurses, hospital administrators—bungled the matter and turned it into an epidemic.

But where did SARS come from? Or AIDS? Or genetic disease? Or treacherous tectonic plates? Or typhoons?

Who's managing this planet, anyhow? Have any of us witnessed divine wisdom in such a way that we can honestly rest in it—trusting that God knows best and will do what's best? Again, I'm pushing here for more than a knee-jerk reply. All our deep-honed creedal instincts, nurtured by hymn and sermon, grandmother's piety and granddad's patriotism, want to rush in and affirm that of course we believe this about God. Of course He is all wise. Of course He knows what to do and when to do it and how to do it, and of course He will do it. Of course.

But it's one thing to say that it's so and another to live like it is.

Often, I'm asked by people in my church to fill out character references for them. Sometimes these references are for people applying for jobs that involve working closely with children. Once in a while, they are for people hoping to adopt a child. The people who ask me to do this are good people, people of integrity, discipline, grace. I usually whip through the form. *Describe how this person handles stress.*

"With calmness and patience." *Describe how this person behaves with their own children.* "She is a caring and attentive mother, stern when she needs to be, but fair...."

I skate through those questions, blithely strewing my answers.

But there's one question, always at the end, that gives me pause. It makes me tremble. It causes me to put down my pen and really think and test my convictions and see if I believe in my heart what I speak with my mouth. The question is, "Would you entrust your own children to this person's care?"

Adam. Sarah. Nicola. Twelve, ten, and seven. My children. Some nights, I lie in bed beside my son Adam and we listen to hockey games. His clock radio bristles with static, and at times it's hard to hear, but it doesn't matter. We're both just looking for an excuse to draw near, to press the length of our arms together. Some evenings, after my daughters get out of the bath, they each in turn sit on my knee, and I brush their hair, slowly and gently, with little tugging, jabbing strokes at first to work out the knots, and then with long, sweeping strokes to give it luster.

My children. The ones I would gladly give my own life for. The ones I would fight with all my strength to defend, and cultivate all tenderness to protect. The ones I love.

Would I entrust Adam and Sarah and Nicola to this person's care? It's not a question I've ever answered glibly. And that's the rub. This is the trick question, the lie detector, the one that pins me to the wall and forces me to declare what I *really think*. It's easy to praise someone's character from afar. But when you're called upon to place your priceless and irreplaceable treasures in that person's hands, you find out what you truly believe.

To the all wise God. Would you entrust your priceless treasures to His wisdom? Would you rest fully in this aspect of His character?

GREEK HAS THREE WORDS for wisdom, and all three are used to describe God's wisdom. The first is *sophia*, from which we get our word *philosophy*. It means insight into the nature of things, an ability to see through, to comprehend truly and fully what is going on. It takes sophia, for instance, to see someone's anger as woundedness, as the mask that they've put over their pain. Sophia is not deceived by surfaces, not duped by disguises.

The second Greek word is *phronesis*. Phronesis is insight applied: taking the ability to see through—sophia—and doing the right thing in light of it. Sometimes we have sophia but lack phronesis, and so a moment of wisdom gives way to folly. We may know, *This angry person before me is really in pain*. That's sophia. But phronesis is the decision: I need to quiet them with my love, and not match fire for fire. Many times, sophia is squandered by a failure of phronesis. They must be married to produce the fullness of wisdom.

That brings us to the third Greek word, *sunesis*. Sunesis, often translated "understanding," describes this marriage, this joining of sophia with phronesis. Sunesis is knowing truth *and* acting on it.

To the only wise God. The Bible's claim is that God possesses all these dimensions of wisdom in completeness and perfection—God embodies all wisdom.

But here's the catch: God has hidden His wisdom from the wise and the learned, and revealed it to little children.[8] By design, God disguises His wisdom, and often the disguise is foolishness.

This is especially true in two of the three showcases God has chosen to display His wisdom. One showcase—creation—is obvious. Creation shows off divine wisdom, if not flawlessly, then with panache, with chutzpah, for all eyes to see. But there are two other showcases for God's wisdom, and these conceal it as much as reveal it. It takes an abiding intimacy with the Father through the Son and in the Spirit to see His wisdom in the other two—to see it so clearly that you rest in it deeply.

But more of that later.

For now, let's take the most obvious showcase for God's wisdom first: creation.

> *By wisdom the* LORD *laid the earth's foundations,*
> *by understanding he set the heavens in place;*
> *by his knowledge the deeps were divided*
> *and the clouds let drop the dew.*[9]

Though much seems amiss in the creation—SARS! AIDS! earthquakes!—the wonder of creation—its infinite bigness, its infinitesimally small detail, its staggering beauty, its harrowing ugliness—is astounding. The simplest things, from worms and stones to eyebrows and fingernails, involve a magnitude of genius humans can admire but never fully imitate. Consider:

> The human body is composed of nearly 100 trillion cells. Think of the skin—while water penetrates the skin outwardly, it cannot penetrate it inwardly. Think of the bones—capable of carrying a load thirty times greater than brick will support. Think of the liver—it breaks up old blood cells into bile and neutralizes poisonous substances. Think of the blood—ten to twelve pints of a syrupy substance that distributes oxygen and carries away waste from tissues and organs, and also regulates the body's temperature. Think of the heart—weighing less than a pound, it's a real workhorse. On the average, it pumps 100,000

times every day, circulating 2,000 gallons of blood through 60,000 miles of arteries, capillaries and veins.[10]

Have you ever tried to create something? Anything—a birdhouse, a go-cart, a cake, a violin? One mistake—a wrong measurement, an extra part, a missed ingredient—and everything else usually goes awry. And how frustrating, even without mistakes, just to get all the parts to work together—dovetails to fit snugly, soufflés to puff without burning, gears to mesh without grinding or release without sticking. And creating things is time-consuming, a vast temporal pit that devours minutes, hours, days, years. The wheel? Centuries of brooding and fumbling, trial and error, failure upon failure. And after all that, even our most dazzling and innovative works—rocket ships or submarines, tennis balls (I'm not kidding) or zippers—are nothing compared to a single leaf on a single tree in God's creation.

As I mentioned, I recently took up scuba diving. Scuba equipment, over many decades of refining, has attained a high level of durability, reliability, functionality, and simplicity. But it's still unwieldy. The outfit—a constricting rubber suit, a spine-twisting tank, a ganglion of hoses, an armload of valves and gauges—is the best design arrived at to date. But held against the simple elegance of a single guppy, it's gaudy and gangling beyond belief.

Creation is God's first showcase for His wisdom.

🕊 🕊 🕊

HIS SECOND SHOWCASE—and where God hides His wisdom as much as unveils it—is the church.

The Bible puts it this way: God's intent "was that now, through the church, the manifold wisdom of God should be made known to the rulers and authorities in the heavenly realms."[11]

The church? This ragtag bunch of squabbling, bumbling, rumor-mongering misfits? Are you kidding? If the church is a showcase of God's wisdom, how wise is that?

Charles Colson opens his book *The Body* with a story about a large and wealthy suburban church that sat next door to a rescue mission. The church, through legal maneuvers, forced the mission to close its doors. The problem? Some of the men and women the mission was trying to help kept wandering over onto the church's beautiful property, smoking in the parking lot, sleeping in the stairwells, littering behind the manicured shrubs, sullying up the place.[12]

The church, rather than being a testimony of God's wisdom, sometimes looks like God's Big Blunder. I once asked my own congregation how many of them had ever been hurt by the church. The air bristled like a staked pit with all the arms that went up. And I know many of these stories. The fistfight that broke out between two deacons at an annual business meeting. The small posse that split and shattered a healthy, thriving church. The acts of blackmail, the hijackings, the lawsuits, the rumor mills, the gossip-mongering, the personality cults, the factions, the scandals, the squabbles, and the many sordid sundry tales of sexual hanky-panky and financial skullduggery. It's enough to make you think that the church is the very worst evidence of God's wisdom.

But the Bible insists that the church makes known God's manifold wisdom. Two things are of crucial importance about this. The first is that it is God's *intent* that through the church His manifold wisdom should be made known.

God *intends* for us to be a testimony to His wisdom. But He leaves us the responsibility of whether or not we'll fulfill or thwart His intent. On Sundays, you make a choice whether you'll *go* to church. But every day, you make a choice whether you'll *be* the church—working out your salvation with fear and trembling, contributing to the health of the whole body, being salt and light, letting no unwholesome word come out of your mouth, having clean hands and a pure heart, loving the least of these. God has not left us to our own devices about this: He freely gives His own wisdom and strength and presence to carry out His intention.

Recently, our church said good-bye to our patron saint, Helen Baker. Helen, nearing eighty and growing frail, was moving away to live with her daughter in another town. Helen never really warmed up to the music at our church. If she had her druthers, we would have sung only hymns in three-quarters time. But she never once complained about it. The week before she moved, someone asked her why she supported this church, year in, year out. She was surprised by the question. "I came here with my husband when he was alive. We became members. We made a promise. We said we would commit to supporting this church. Why wouldn't we keep that promise?"

It's God's *intent* that His wisdom would be made known through the church.

The second crucial thing is that God's wisdom through the church is made known "to the rulers and authorities in the heavenly realms."

The drama of our lives is cosmic more than earthly, not intended primarily for human eyes. The church's chief witness is heaven-bent, vertical rather than horizontal, played out in the presence of demons and angels more than neighbors and colleagues. God's wisdom is refracted through the church, but mere mortals sit cockeyed to it, at an angle that eclipses rather than emblazons it. It's like looking into water: At too close an angle, its surface obscures its depths; only at higher levels does the surface magnify the beauty and intricacy beneath it. To see the church's wisdom fully, in all its many-layered, jewel-like splendor, you have to be higher up. What is foolishness to man, when seen from the right perspective, is the very wisdom of God.

God's ways, seen at ground level, are often puzzling, both to ourselves and to those who gather near. We fumble for explanations, scramble to find some account for why things are the way they are, and still we come up with nothing more than blandishments and balderdash.

God, it turns out, does not stage His wisdom show for *our* friends or enemies. He stages it for *His*—"the rulers and authorities in the heavenly realms." They get front-row seats. They witness His wisdom through the church.

And what do they see? That God takes the most unlikely people—not many of whom are wise by human standards[13]—and by sheer grace and at great cost, makes them His very own. God adopts riffraff and ragamuffins:

> He chose the lowly things of this world and the despised things—and the things that are not—to nullify the things that are.... It is because of him that you are in Christ Jesus, who has become for us wisdom from God— that is, our righteousness, holiness and redemption.[14]

The wisdom of God that we can rest in is not first or foremost a demonstration of creative brilliance or managerial competency or technical mastery. It is, rather, wisdom disguised as foolishness. It is not aptitudinal, but relational; not a display of divine proficiency, but an unveiling of the Father's heart toward the least of these. Jesus *becomes* wisdom for us.

He does in us, through us, and on our behalf what we could never do for ourselves. In a move so reckless and costly and counterintuitive it seems harebrained and laughable to the so-called philosophers of this age,[15] but which makes the rulers and authorities in the heavenly places shudder, God sought those who were nothing and made them, by His choice, His own sons and daughters.

God's wisdom is this: He chose you and me for no better reason than because He *wants* us for His own. That's enough for me to rest in.

WHICH LEADS TO THE LAST, best thing. The main show-case of God's wisdom is neither the creation nor the church.

It is the Cross.

> For the message of the cross is foolishness to those who are perishing, but to us who are being saved it is the power of God.[16]

Imagine if God assembled the world's experts to help Him answer the question, "How do you deal with sin and evil?"

The Philosopher would speak: "God, it is my considered opinion that we must apply rigorous logic to the problem. It's really an intellectual deficiency. Send them teachers,

Socratic-like teachers, men with minds illumined by deep thoughts, whose tongues are blessed with eloquence. Make it dignified. Lofty. Bring the consolation of philosophy. Educate them out of their trouble."

The Moralist stands up: "Mr. God, with all due respect, these people need to strive after the good life more robustly, more vigorously. They need to be more circumspect in the way they live. I think You need to devise a carefully calibrated system of reward and punishment and make them earn, by good deeds, their way into heaven."

The Politician interrupts: "No, God. It's policy reform. That's what's needed." And the Militarist finally storms in, gruff with impatience: "Policy reform! God, You simply need to go kick butt. Mobilize the troops. We're gonna do this thing big, just like Iraq. They won't know what hit 'em."

"Hah!" the Entertainer shouts. "They're all wrong, God. What You really need to do is razzle-dazzle them. Lots of music, stunts. Blow up some cars and buildings. Show them power! We can pipe in a Dolby digital soundtrack. Generate some computer graphics. We'll get Peter Jackson to direct. It will be a spectacle!"

And on and on would go the wisdom of the world. And you and I? We'd still be in our sin. Dying, dying, dying.

God didn't consult our wisdom. God said, "This is how I will save them. I will come Myself, in disguise. I'll be born in a barn to an unmarried couple. I will live in obscurity for thirty years, then wander like a vagabond, slum around with a rag-tag group of men who are rash one minute, timid the next. I will live in poverty. I will make enemies of the powerful and the influential. I will go to Jerusalem, straight into their snare, and be beaten. I will be killed like a criminal."

From then until now, the pundits and experts have looked on and, like the Stoic and Epicurean philosophers who listened to Paul speak on this subject in Athens, asked, "What is this babbler trying to say?"[17]

For the message of the Cross is foolishness to those who are perishing.

But a few, then and now, see beneath the disguise, that here is true wisdom—the wisdom that doesn't just talk, but that acts, acts with power to save even a wretch like me. *To us who are being saved it is the power of God.*

The book of 1 Kings tells of the great wisdom of Solomon and offers one story to illustrate it. Two women come to the king, each claiming to be the mother of the same baby. Solomon says, "I can't tell who's the real mother. Bring me a sword. Cut this child in two, and give half to each woman." One woman cries, "Do it!" The other cries, "No, give the child to her." Solomon knows instantly who the real mother is: the one who would give the child away. That's wisdom, knowing that love would rather see its child alive and whole in someone else's arms than dead and dismembered in its own.[18]

The wisdom of God puts a new twist on this. God wanted

to see us alive and whole in *His* arms, but sin was killing us. Sin was the sword that would sever us.

So the King had Himself cut in two instead.

It took the Son of Man, the Son of God, dying on a cross to make us whole and to get us back into the Father's arms. With all the wisdom in the world, we never would have figured that out. But when we see it, when we grasp it, we boast in nothing else. We trust in no one else. At the cross God made a way, and you and I can rest there for all eternity.

To Him, the only wise God, be glory forever through Jesus Christ.

Chapter Eleven

THE GIFT
WE REFUSE

God's Rest

Tom Hanks made a movie a few years ago called *Cast Away*. It's a modern Robinson Crusoe story. Tom plays Chuck Noland, a paunchy, snippy FedEx executive. His job is to make sure overnight packages funnel through the courier service with the fewest possible hitches and glitches, the highest degree of seamless efficiency. It must be on time! Chuck's life is driven by the clock. Every gesture—even proposing marriage to his girlfriend—is bound by a rigid and relentless schedule. He tosses her an engagement ring as he leaps from his car to a plane headed for Malaysia.

He never gets to his destination. A rogue storm rises up and flings his plane hundreds of miles off course, and then hurls it into a dark sea. Everyone but Chuck Noland dies. He washes up on a tiny desert island. Thus begins the longest, deepest interruption of Chuck's life. For four years, he's a castaway, forgotten, unsought. He lives in utter aloneness, except for a volleyball—"Wilson"—that becomes his mute confidant and soul mate. Chuck dwells in perfect silence, in a world reduced to day and night, sea and sky, sun and moon. He skewers fish with a whittled branch, snares crab in a makeshift trap, kindles fire by rubbing sticks together. He grows bronze-skinned and shaggy, sinewy and nimble. He lives in timelessness.

Watching the film, I was surprised that my dominant emotion was not pity. It was envy. Envy of the stillness, the solitude, the world without clocks, deadlines, appointments, schedules, obligations. The rest.

Chuck eventually gets off the island and returns to the world of time. People have moved on without him, hardly even pausing to say good-bye. *There's no time for that.* Always moving, but never changing.

But Chuck stopped. He rested. And it transforms him. He sees everything in a new way, holds it with his hands held open. The movie ends with Chuck standing at a crossroads, each road stretching as far as the eye can see. He is relaxed, smiling, in no hurry. His whole body is light. He is poised, effortless, between boundless opportunity, endless discovery. He can go anywhere, or nowhere. He can become anything he chooses.[1]

And I envied him.

Then I talked with a man who had been a hard-driven

and hard-driving financial kingpin. He had no time for friends, family, worship, play. Then he had a heart attack.

He was forced to stop, to rest.

The world, of course, moved on without him. Stocks were bought and sold, profits were gained and lost, deals were made and broken. People continued to meet for lunch, to gossip about those who weren't present. His name might have been mentioned: "Did you hear about Al?" "Yeah, an aneurysm, wasn't it?" "I'm not sure. I heard a stroke." "Poor sap." "Yeah."

That heart attack was the best thing that ever happened to him. That's what he told me. He began to spend time with his wife, his children, his neighbors. He learned to eat bread with grains and seeds kneaded in, fruit with its skin still on, juice with a thickness of pulp still in it. He started walking, noticing things—the shape of leaves, the texture of stones, the sounds of springtime, the fragrance of his daughter's skin. He learned the names of plants. He took up woodcarving.

And I envied him.

You know you're in serious trouble when the people you start to envy are castaways and cardiac patients.

ONE OF THE TRIUMPHS of the cult of busyness is that most of us feel guilty for stopping. Efficiency is our fetish, production our worship. If you're not producing, and quickly, what good are you? How can you justify your existence without busyness? How can you account for your being if not on the ledger of your doing?

But it's killing us. There is only one story in all Scripture that gives any clear indication of the kind of activity God forbids on the Sabbath. That may surprise you if you grew up in a church that had lots of rules about Sabbath-keeping. The Bible has virtually no rules, only general guidelines: cease work, bear no load, feast, celebrate, seek refreshment, take a rest.

But there is this one story, told in Numbers:

> While the Israelites were in the desert, a man was found gathering wood on the Sabbath day. Those who found him gathering wood brought him to Moses and Aaron and the whole assembly, and they kept him in custody, because it was not clear what should be done to him. Then the LORD said to Moses, "The man must die. The whole assembly must stone him outside the camp." So the assembly took him outside the camp and stoned him to death, as the LORD commanded Moses.[2]

The punishment seems grossly out of proportion to the crime. Gather wood and die. And yet, the man won't stop. He won't, for one day, lay down his load and refuse to pick it up again. He won't, for one day, trust God to meet his needs.

Such living always carries with it a death penalty. It bloats the ego, wizens the soul, hardens the heart. It is the way of grasping, which always, by its very nature, leaves us unable to receive. Jesus warned us about this. He admonished us not to chase after more and more, to fret over what we'll eat, what we'll wear. That's how pagans live, He said, how those without God get by. Don't do it, Jesus said; it gets you nowhere.

Or worse, it kills you.

"THERE IS ASTOUNDING WISDOM in the traditional Jewish Sabbath," theologian Wayne Muller writes:

> Sabbath is not dependent upon our readiness to stop. We do not stop [because] we are finished. We do not stop [because] we [have] complete[d] our phone calls, finish[ed] our project, [gotten] through this stack of messages, or [sent] out this report that is due tomorrow. We stop because it is time to stop.... *Sabbath liberates us from the need to be finished.* The old wise Sabbath says: Stop now.[3]

There is a time for everything, the book of Ecclesiastes reminds us. There is a time to work, but there is a time to stop work. Sabbath is the time to stop.

And if we don't, we discover soon enough what the writer of Ecclesiastes knew: Our work, no matter how significant and extravagant, becomes a sour and wearisome business, toilsome, meaningless, fruitless.

The old, wise Sabbath says, *Stop now.*

God stopped and rested. Indeed, that is the first and best reason that we should stop and rest.

> "Remember the Sabbath day by keeping it holy. Six days you shall labor and do all your work, but the seventh day is a Sabbath to the LORD your God. On it you shall not do any work, neither you, nor your son or daughter, nor your manservant or maidservant, nor your animals, nor the alien within your gates. For in six days the LORD made the heavens and the earth, the sea, and all that is in them, but he rested on the seventh day. Therefore the LORD blessed the Sabbath day and made it holy."[4]

Sabbath is a time to remember and observe and celebrate and anticipate. We remember God's deliverance of His people from slavery and bondage. We celebrate Jesus' triumph over death and sin through His resurrection. We anticipate the day when we will enter into the fullness of Sabbath rest in heaven, with all the saints gathered in worship in the very presence of our God.

Sabbath, in other words, is largely about delighting in those things that only God can do, only God can bring about. We can't deliver ourselves or resurrect ourselves or get ourselves to heaven. These things God alone can do. Sabbath is the day when we remember that, observe that, and celebrate that.

But God blessed the Sabbath and made it holy first and foremost because that's the day He stopped and rested. So although keeping Sabbath is a principal way we remember, observe, and celebrate those things that God alone can do, it doesn't begin there. It begins, rather, when we imitate the one thing that God alone *did not have to do.* He did not have to stop. He did not have to rest.

But we do. All living things do. And so God led the way. He stopped, He rested, and then He invited us to do likewise. *Sabbath is imitating God's own rest in order that we might become more like God and yet know that we are not God.*

Our refusal to stop usually stems from getting this exactly backward. We won't dare imitate God's own rest because we are too busy trying to *be* God. Who will run the world, if not me? Who will provide? How will the bills get paid? Who will preach next week? How will things hold together if my hands aren't holding them? I am so busy with the work of deliverance and resurrection and getting people to heaven—I am so busy *being* God—I have no time to be *like* God. *God, if You want a day off, that's Your business. But You can see very well that I have no time for such frivolity.*

But God stopped. God rested. What greater example do we need? And God says, "Stop! Rest!" What stronger motivation do we need? God says, "Stop, rest, and I will make you to be more like Me." How much more attractive an incentive do we need?

I cherish a story about Martin Luther and his friend Philipp Melanchthon. Melanchthon was the scholar in the partnership, the pedant who relished finespun debate over theological intricacies. Luther, on the other hand, was forever the rough-hewn peasant, the earthy, ale-loving rabble-rouser who managed somehow to be the devil's advocate and the devil's archenemy all in one.

One morning Melanchthon announced to Luther, "Today, you and I shall discuss the governance of the universe."

Luther looked at him with, I imagine, an expression of scorn hiding mirth. "No, my friend," he said. "Today, you and I will go fishing. We'll leave the governance of the universe to God."[5]

SABBATH IS A GIFT of the restful God to His restless people. It is a statutory holiday, a King's birthday, bestowed on us weekly. That ever we should have come to resent it—to see it as a burden God laid on us rather than a way He eases our burden, to see it as a day He stole from us rather than one He lavishes on us—is bizarre beyond reckoning.

Take a day off! is the message of Sabbath. Relax. Sleep in. Take a midday nap. Play. Party. Eat. Dance. Be like children.

How dare You, God! I can't believe You would do such a thing. Harrumph!

I remember a marvelous scene near the end of Charles Dickens's *A Christmas Carol,* in which the old skinflint and taskmaster Scrooge finally stops. It takes a disaster to make him stop. He's got to be blown hundreds of miles off course and brought to the edge of his own grave. But finally Scrooge stops, and he is transformed and set free.

Now it is the morning after Christmas. Scrooge is a new man. He woke Christmas Day brimful with joy, spilling with benediction, in a spirit of revelry and bounty. He spent the day blessing and giving. But this is the next day, and he's back in his office, hunched over his books vulturelike. Scrooge had grudgingly allowed his poor, haggard employee Bob Cratchit to take Christmas Day off, but demanded that Cratchit be in all the earlier the next day.

Cratchit comes in eighteen minutes late. He is flustered, nervous, and quickly settles into his desk.

"Mr. Cratchit!" Scrooge's stern, hard voice booms from the shadows.

"Y-y-yes, sir?" Cratchit answers, quavering.

"What do you mean by coming here at this time of day?"

Cratchit starts to apologize, to explain.

"I'll tell you what, my friend, I am not going to stand this sort of thing any longer," Scrooge says. "You leave me no choice...but to raise your salary."

Scrooge starts to giggle.

"A merry Christmas, Bob," says Scrooge, with an earnestness that cannot be mistaken, as he claps him on the back. "A merrier Christmas, Bob, my good fellow, than I have given you for many a year. And I want you to let me help your struggling family. Let us discuss your affairs this very afternoon, over a Christmas bowl of smoking bishop, Bob."

Cratchit stands agog. Has his old boss gone mad? But then he realizes that Scrooge means it, and he himself is caught up in his master's joy.

But imagine if he weren't. Imagine that Cratchit resented Scrooge for his generosity. Imagine that and you've captured the absurdity of our own thinking about God's gift of rest. *You leave Me no choice,* God says, *but to raise your salary. And now, come, let's enjoy ourselves together.*

This is a gift.

꩜ ꩜ ꩜

BUT SOMEWHERE WE LOST the gift beneath our lists. This is maybe the primary mistake we make when we try to figure out the Sabbath: We go straight to the rules. What can I do, what can't I do? Can I garden? shop? play football?

This is the pharisaical tendency, to concoct rule upon rule and, in a mechanical, dutiful way, try to fulfill them. In Jesus' day, the religious leaders had buried Sabbath-keeping beneath a thick crust of strict and finicky regulations. They'd lost the gift beneath their lists.

Jesus repeatedly broke their rules for just that reason. He wanted to shock us into the awareness that keeping Sabbath is not about keeping rules; it's about recovering God's heart, His passion and compassion, His desire for people to be all they were created to be.

The Pharisee has a question: What is lawful on the Sabbath? But that's the wrong question. This is the right one: *What is the essence of the Sabbath?*

Jesus said, "The Sabbath was made for man, not man for the Sabbath."[6] That doesn't mean we are free to abuse it. It doesn't mean we can take it or leave it. "If you keep your feet from breaking the Sabbath and from *doing as you please* on my holy day," God declares through the prophet Isaiah, "if you call the Sabbath a delight...and if you honor it *by not going your own way and not doing as you please*...then you will find your joy in the LORD."[7] The Sabbath is made for us, but that doesn't mean we can treat it as we please, any more than the fact that your house was made for you means you can trash it.

It means we dare not lose the gift beneath our lists.

I love going to Vancouver's Stanley Park. There are so many things to explore there—the rose gardens, the sandy beaches and rocky shores, the seawall, the water park, the forest trails, the lakes and lagoons, the cliffs and fields, the aquarium, the wide-open lawn where artisans lay out their wares. My family and I often spend a day there. We walk, we sit, we play, we talk, we laugh. That park was made for man, not man for the park. It was made for people, but that doesn't give me or anyone else license to trample it.

I don't go to Stanley Park with the question *What is lawful?* uppermost in my mind. *Can I kill squirrels? Can I swim with the dolphins? Can I chop down trees?* That would completely miss the point. I would lose the gift beneath my lists.

No, I go to Stanley Park and think, *Wow! Look at this place! All these wonders, all this beauty I can explore. And it's all mine!*

Can I shop on the Sabbath? Can I work on my car? Can I finish my business report?

Losing the gift beneath the lists.

Here is how we ought to enter the Sabbath: *Wow! Look at this day! I can play, sing, sleep, dance a jig, kiss my wife, tussle with my kids, eat a feast. And it's all mine.*

It's a gift, just for you.

THE LATE ACTOR Hume Cronyn made a movie once with Alfred Hitchcock. Hitchcock was notorious for his fiddling, meddlesome ways in moviemaking. He endlessly tweaked, tinkered, polished, and he could be ruthlessly demanding with his actors. So it was a surprise to Cronyn what happened this one day:

> We were working on a problem with a scene. There were a lot of things to consider—lighting, staging, pacing, and the like. We were up very late struggling to find the right way to do it. Finally, when we seemed close to the solution, Hitchcock...started telling jokes, silly, junior high–type stuff, and got us all lost again. Later, I asked him why, when we were so close to solving the problem, did he choose that moment to get us off track by joking around? He paused, and then said something I'll never forget. He said, "You were pushing. It never comes from pushing."[8]

It never comes from pushing. There are some things that only grow in stillness—or silliness—that only flourish in rest, or laughter. No one plants a garden and then keeps plowing the ground. You have to wait. You have to let things lie still, let seeds break open and spin their roots downward, push their stems upward. You have to let earth and sky and rain do what only they can do.

It's no different with us. Most of the things we need in order to be most fully alive never come from pushing. They grow in rest. Kindness, joy, compassion, friendship, courage, hope, trust, understanding. These are essential to character and community. Yet none of them takes root in busyness and striving. They tend, rather, to wither under those conditions. Endless busyness disturbs the roots of virtue and, instead, breeds suspicion, anger, frustration, despair, cowardice, loneliness. Without some way of replenishing the virtues, we easily become weary in doing good.

God made a man. He put him to work in the garden, to plow, to prune, to harvest, to name. All was good. Very good. Except one thing: The man was alone. It was not good for him to be alone. It was, in fact, the first and deepest problem in the universe, a personal crisis that marred the whole of creation.

How do you solve a problem like that? "The LORD God caused the man to fall into a deep sleep; and while he was sleeping, he took one of the man's ribs and closed up the place with flesh. Then the LORD God made a woman from the rib he had taken out of the man."[9]

The answer to the man's deepest need and longing came

from within the man, but it was not available to the man through his own efforts. God had to draw it out of him while he slept. He had to cease. He had to rest.

It never comes from pushing.

⚜ ⚜ ⚜

I READ ABOUT A MOTHER whose son was hyperactive with an attention deficit. She tried everything to change him, to calm him. Drugs. Therapy. Discipline. All failed. Finally, in utter desperation, she grabbed her son one day in the mayhem of one his eruptions and held him in a tight and loving embrace, singing, speaking words of consolation and affection to him, pressing his head to her chest, rocking him. He thrashed, twisted, squirmed.

Then he quieted. He rested in his mother's arms. And when she set him down, the peace lasted. Now every time he has an outburst, this is what she does—holds him until she quiets him.

"I do it long enough," she says, "for him to remember who he is."[10]

Sabbath is God holding you long enough for you to remember who you are: not God, but one whose life is in His hands, the hands of the One who wants to give you good gifts.

Chapter Twelve

BEAUTY IN THE CREVICE

God's Glory

Brian Kelly wanted to leave this earth in a burst of glory. Literally. He died and was cremated in July 1994. His instructions were for his body's ashes to be mixed with gunpowder and packed into a canister-sized firework shell, twelve inches in diameter. On August 12, 1994, at a convention of pyrotechnicians in Pittsburgh, Brian Kelly—reduced to two pounds of gray, silky dust— was hurled heavenward, spiraling into the night sky with two silvery comet tails looping behind, where he erupted in thunder and starburst, a cannonade of booms, a cascade of brilliant colors.

And then all was blackness.

I guess it's a kind of glory.

When I think of glory, though, I think of September 28, 1972, the day of the last game of the first Canada/USSR hockey series. For those of us who grew up in Canada, with its terrible wild beauty, its dizzying bigness, its despotic winter cruelty, its excess of geography and climate—nothing done by halves—this was one of the highest moments of patriotism. This was our Boston Tea Party.

It's the eighth and final game. Canada leads the series but needs this game to clinch it. Otherwise, the series is a draw, four games apiece. The game is tied, five to five, less than a minute remaining. And the game is being played in Moscow, in Mordor, deep behind enemy lines, in front of a crowd that hisses like asps at our team, that howls for their own team with the frenzy and savagery of bloodlust. The referee, rumor has it, has been given orders from the Kremlin itself to sew up this game for Team USSR. And he's doing just that, playing favorites like a fairy-tale stepmother, nitpicking with the Canadians, indulgent toward the Russians. Both teams are exhausted, reckless with weariness. All play has gone out of the sport. It is pure battle.

I am in sixth grade at the time, watching the game from the teacher's lounge in my little school. Those who have finished their classroom work early have been allowed to watch, and never before and never again has the motivation to do our work been so powerful. I've never been much of a hockey fan, but this is different. This is us against the Russians. The world is in the deep freeze of the Cold War, the democratic, freedom-loving West pitted against the communist, atheistic East. This is war by other means. This is *Realpolotik*. This is standing astride a historical fault line as it starts to heave and shift, no telling what it will swallow or thrust up, what monuments it will topple, how unrecognizable it will render the landscape. The series has taken on mythic proportions. It's a passion play, a Greek tragedy.

An apocalypse.

And all depends on us.

Paul Henderson is playing right wing. He's had a mediocre career up until now, but he's played brilliantly in this series, his skating a blend of kickboxing and ballet, his stick work a kind of sleight-of-hand trickery, like tae kwon do. He is fast and smart and lethal. With the clock running out, Henderson takes a pass, weaves his way to the net, and shoots. The Russian goalie, Vladislav Tretiak, easily deflects it. But Tretiak doesn't get hold of the puck. It skitters back onto the ice. Henderson, with thirty-six seconds left on the clock, picks it up again.

This time he doesn't miss.

In Canada, a shout goes up that's heard around the world. Thirty-four seconds later, the game is over, and every man, woman, and child in our country, coast to coast, breaks out in our national anthem, "O Canada!" and sings it with pride so huge it makes our marrow ache.

Glory!

꒰ ꒰ ꒰

BUT THAT'S NOTHING.

This is something: God's glory.

Indeed, all our spectacles, our moments in the sun, our heroism, our conquest—all are the merest hints of His splendor. Our glory is dim—a spattering of light, then darkness. God's glory is brilliant—a radiance so huge, so intense, that it burns up even the shadows it might otherwise cast. Our glory is fleeting—thunderous applause that dwindles to a musty nostalgia, in time to the silence of forgetting.

But God's glory is a whisper that gathers and crescendos to a cosmos-shaking, eternally sustained *Hallelujah!*

Take the most glorious sight you've ever beheld—a moment when your heart was surging to the point of bursting, when every ounce of you shimmered, every inch of you brimmed—and multiply that a millionfold. And still all you have is the slightest echo, the faintest glint, of God's eternal glory. One day we will see it. One day, we will have hearts and eyes prepared to see it.

One day.

But not yet. Not now. Now we can't even imagine it. Now beholding its unveiled splendor would consume us. We could sooner walk barefoot on the sun. We could more easily swallow the ocean. It's too much.

So for now, His glory comes disguised.

꒱ ꒱ ꒱

THE WHOLE EARTH IS FULL OF GOD'S GLORY. The first time I read this in Isaiah, the eternal song of the six-winged seraphim, it puzzled me. It disappointed me. *The whole earth is full of God's glory? It is? Where? How?*

I've seen glimmers of it. I've heard rumors of it. But the *whole earth filled* with it? Doesn't this overstate the matter? Doesn't it smack of marketing hyperbole? I can accept that all *heaven* is filled with God's glory. I can accept that *the whole earth* has shards of that glory, a thin pulse of it like the galactic aftershock of a distant exploding sun. I can accept that upon the earth, *here and there,* in corners, in crevices, in this church, in that home, God's glory shines with a clear, pure brightness.

But the whole earth full of it? What I couldn't grasp were the volumes, the dimensions. Like Mary, when the angel Gabriel told her she was to bear the God-child, I wondered at this and pondered it in my heart and dared to ask, "How could this be?"

꒱ ꒱ ꒱

I BEGAN TO FIND MY ANSWER on the flank of a remote, austere mountain, dark with storm, alongside a man weary from doing good.

This was Moses' second encounter with God on Mount

Sinai. In his first encounter, he went up the mountain to receive the Law, hewing and hauling two stone tablets with him so that God could inscribe them with His finger. While he was gone, the Israelites became restless, surly. A splinter of discontent grew to riotous, mutinous proportions. They were ready to burn the house down. They were spoiling to lynch the leaders.

God had shown mercy and faithfulness to these people in spectacular ways: He rescued them from slavery, routed their enemies, fed them, guided them, protected them. He had been a pillar of fire for them at night, light and warmth in the dark, cold wasteland. He had been a pillar of cloud for them in the day, shade from the wanton desert sun. And now God had provided the Law. This was to be the bedrock and the crucible for life together. It was to anchor and shape them as pilgrims and worshipers, as a people set apart. The Ten Commandments, though carved in rock, expressed God's heart.

But the people wanted more. They wanted something new, something old, something that gratified their craving for novelty and at the same time satisfied their nostalgia for the past. They wanted what they used to have, and what all the other nations around them had.

They wanted an idol.

Moses' brother Aaron, the man left in charge, was just the guy to serve it up. He was a combination of daring initiative and cowardly reaction, of entrepreneurial sharpness and spiritual dullness. *All these people need,* he reasoned, *is a spiritual experience to distract them, to placate them.* So he got the people to throw their gold into a fire, and he fashioned a calf from it. Then he led the people to worship it.

God was angry, so angry He wanted to destroy the people, and Moses had to intervene on their behalf. Moses stood in the gap, as Psalm 106 puts it, and argued God down. God relented, but He was still angry and threatened to simply abandon the people—they could make their own way from here. No more manna. No more miracles. No more pillars of fire and cloud.

This is where I found my answer about God's glory, standing beside this man who was weary of doing good. Moses has won the first round of argument with the Lord. God concedes that He will not destroy the people, but He insists on forsaking them. So Moses presses in for round two—he wants all of God or nothing:

> Moses said to the LORD, "You have been telling me, 'Lead these people,' but you have not let me know whom you will send with me. You have said, 'I know you by name and you have found favor with me.' If you are pleased with me, teach me your ways so I may know you and continue to find favor with you. Remember that this nation is your people."

The LORD replied, "My Presence will go with you, and I will give you rest."

Then Moses said to him, "If your Presence does not go with us, do not send us up from here. How will anyone know that you are pleased with me and with your people unless you go with us? What else will distinguish me and your people from all the other people on the face of the earth?"

And the LORD said to Moses, "I will do the very thing you have asked, because I am pleased with you and I know you by name."[1]

Moses isn't distressed about losing the provisions of God. He is distressed only about losing the presence of God. *If your Presence does not go with us, do not send us up from here. What else will distinguish me and your people from all the other people on the face of the earth?*

This is the core question of every disciple. It is every Christian leader's question. It is every church's question. *What else but God's presence will distinguish me and Your people from everyone else on the face of the earth?*

Nothing. Nothing will. Nothing can. If I speak with the tongues of men and angels, but God's presence does not go with me, what else will distinguish me from just another orator? If the church is involved—and she must be—in social action, in legal reform, in feeding the hungry; if we give our bodies to the flame and have faith to move mountains and to fathom all mysteries, but His presence does not go with us, what else will distinguish us from all the other educational institutions and welfare agencies on the face of the earth?

Nothing.

Anyone can do what we do. Most, in fact, do it better. They have bigger budgets, shrewder marketing, splashier promotion, more streamlined organization. The world's production values make us look like bumpkins and rustics. We are mostly working out of old buildings with water-stained ceilings and rattle-fanned furnaces, with cardboard cartons for filing cabinets and a toilet whose tank cover is permanently removed so you can fiddle the plunger to flush it. I attended a church not long ago where the congregation sat on rickety chairs with stained, threadbare upholstery. The sanctuary was covered in burnt-orange shag carpeting that smelled like a root cellar and bunched like an old sow's hide. The music was squawky and shrill. The preacher seemed weary, harried, a tad angry.

And yet there was a joy and expectancy in the place that nothing that met the eye—nothing that met any of the senses—could account for. These people were either deluded or they knew a deep secret.

All that really distinguishes us from all the other people on the face of the earth is that God is with us.

🦅 🦅 🦅

GOD AGREES WITH MOSES. Only His presence can distinguish these people. So He will go with them.

If I were Moses, I'd stop there. That's enough and don't press your advantage. But Moses—out of wisdom or folly or just old-fashioned pluck and stubbornness—dares to ask for one more thing.

Moses said, "Now show me your glory."

What happens next is critical. It is the Rosetta stone for understanding how the whole earth is full of God's glory.

> And the LORD said, "I will cause all my goodness to pass in front of you, and I will proclaim my name, the LORD, in your presence. I will have mercy on whom I will have mercy, and I will have compassion on whom I will have compassion."[2]

God has Moses crawl into a cleft on a mountain bluff, and then:

> The LORD came down in the cloud and stood there with him and proclaimed his name, the LORD. And he passed in front of Moses, proclaiming, "The LORD, the LORD, the com-

passionate and gracious God, slow to anger, abounding in love and faithfulness, maintaining love to thousands, and forgiving wickedness, rebellion and sin. Yet he does not leave the guilty unpunished; he punishes the children and their children for the sin of the fathers to the third and fourth generation."[3]

What is the glory of God on earth? In simplest terms, this: His goodness shown, His name proclaimed. And both those things—His goodness and His name—are summed up in the revelation of His nature.

My friend Bill Jensen calls this passage "God's self-portrait." When Bill first told me that, I thought of Rembrandt's many self-portraits throughout his long career. So much is revealed in the eyes, in the artist's dark, watchful eyes, with their hidden layers of grief and joy, playfulness and wariness. His last self-portrait depicts an old man. His skin is mottled with liver spots. He is rumpled and pale. But the eyes are eloquent. They brim with secrets and rumors, with a deep, wordless knowing. There is sadness there, and wisdom. There is caution, humility, strength. There is vulnerability, as if he's trying to tell you, with just his eyes, that he needs you to stay a little longer, wait with him, dwell in this silence with him, listen, watch. Those eyes plead and promise, invite and warn.

His whole life is present in those eyes.

Moses never sees God's face, not on Sinai. God shows him only His back side. But I think Moses, folded like a bird sheltering in a crease of granite, sees God's eyes. He sees in them the One full of mercy, compassionate and gracious, slow to anger, abounding in love, maintaining love to thousands. The One who is unfailingly just, who does not leave sin unpunished.

His goodness shown, His name proclaimed.

In His eyes, Moses sees God's glory.

THIS IS WHERE IT gets personal. We've been asking, How is the whole earth filled with God's glory? And we've answered, Wherever His name is proclaimed, wherever His goodness is shown, there His glory shines through.

Which means we're it. You and me. We're the ones who either display or eclipse the glory of God. The apostle Paul gets explicit about this. The glory of God, Paul says, is in the gospel of Jesus Christ and the person of Jesus Christ:

> Now if the ministry that brought death, which was engraved in letters on stone, came with glory, so that the Israelites could not look steadily at the face of Moses because of its glory, fading though it was, will not the ministry of the Spirit be even more glorious?

> If the ministry that condemns men is glorious,
> how much more glorious is the ministry that
> brings righteousness! For what was glorious
> has no glory now in comparison with the sur-
> passing glory. And if what was fading away
> came with glory, how much greater is the glory
> of that which lasts![4]

After Moses saw God's glory, he glowed from the intensity of that encounter. It shone in his face. But it also faded, seeped out like water held in the hand. So Moses veiled his face—at first to hide the radiance, but then to hide its diminishment. Either way, the glory had to be covered over.

But not with us:

> Therefore, since we have such a hope, we are
> very bold. We are not like Moses, who would
> put a veil over his face to keep the Israelites
> from gazing at it while the radiance was fad-
> ing away. But their minds were made dull, for
> to this day the same veil remains when the old
> covenant is read. It has not been removed,
> because only in Christ is it taken away. Even
> to this day when Moses is read, a veil covers
> their hearts. But whenever anyone turns to
> the Lord, the veil is taken away. Now the Lord

is the Spirit, and where the Spirit of the Lord is, there is freedom. And we, who with unveiled faces all reflect the Lord's glory, are being transformed into his likeness with ever-increasing glory, which comes from the Lord, who is the Spirit.[5]

Moses saw only God's back, but we know "the glory of God in the face of Christ."[6] Moses had to veil the glory's reflection in his own face, but we're free to walk about with unveiled faces. Moses had to hide the glory's fading, but we're invited to display it openly, as it shines in us with "ever-increasing glory." Moses, every day, became a little more his old self. But we, every day, by the Spirit's work, become a little more like Jesus.

We carry around God's splendor. His name, His nature, His mercy, His justice. This all-surpassing glory.

꙳ ꙳ ꙳

THIS GLORY IS IN US but not from us. Paul goes on:

Therefore, since through God's mercy we have this ministry, we do not lose heart. Rather, we have renounced secret and shameful ways; we do not use deception, nor do we distort the word of God. On the contrary, by setting forth the truth plainly we commend ourselves to every man's conscience in the sight of God. And even if our gospel is veiled, it is veiled to those who are perishing. The god of this age has blinded the minds of unbelievers, so that they cannot see the light of the gospel of the glory of Christ, who is the image of God. For we do not preach ourselves, but Jesus Christ as Lord, and ourselves as your servants for Jesus' sake. For God, who said, "Let light shine out of darkness," made his light shine in our hearts to give us the light of the knowledge of the glory of God in the face of Christ.[7]

And now watch:

But we have this treasure in jars of clay to show that this all-surpassing power is from God and not from us.[8]

We carry His glory in clay jars—fragile, thickset, mundane pots. We carry it in ourselves, these drab, chipped, earthen vessels, prone to crack from pressure, liable to break from dropping, as likely to carry trash as treasure.

How is the whole earth full of God's glory? How does the

world know God's name, His nature, see His mercy, taste His justice? They see it in you and me, or not at all. They see it in our ordinariness transformed, in the way Jesus unveils Himself suddenly in our grief and our joy, our hardship and our windfall, when something of God's goodness breaks out from our plain lives and others see it, even if only its back side, even if only from between a cleft of rock, a tight scrape, a peephole. But it's there, unmistakable.

So if You don't go with us, God, what will distinguish us from all the other people on the face of the earth? All we have, like anyone else, are these clay jar lives. Unless You fill them with Your mercy-loving, justice-doing presence, we are nothing.

But if He does go with us and we stand in His presence, our task is simply to live with unveiled faces. Our work is to keep the clay jars uncovered.

It's what first attracted me to Christians.

As a teen I had one grand obsession: skiing. For a few years, it eclipsed everything else, consumed everything else. My single vision for my life was to ski freestyle professionally. Every weekend, my brother and best friend and I spent Saturday and often Sunday on the slopes, mastering our foot-work in the moguls, honing our agility in ballet, perfecting our technique in aerials. We were three footloose dancers, cocky and brash and full of ourselves.

My brother and I grew up outside the church. But our best friend at the time was a lapsed Christian. His parents were devout, but he was more heathen than my brother or I—he could drink harder, cuss more fervently, chase women with wilder abandon. All of us had mouths that could make an oil rigger blush.

One day we were driving down from Mount Baker in Washington, one of our favorite mountains. A blizzard had been blowing all day, and the narrow, snaking road, no more than a goat trail in places, gleamed blue with ice. The road was banked high on both sides with snowdrifts that the massive plow blades had chiseled into steely walls of ice. I was driving, inching the car down. I could feel, with every nudge of the wheel, every brush of the brakes, the car wanting to slew into a tailspin. I geared down low and tried to do as little braking as possible.

But then we came to a long, straight stretch, and there was no way to avoid the brakes. Otherwise, the car would gather momentum that after a few hundred feet would be murderous. I tried feathering the brakes, just skimming the drums enough to slow us down with the friction. And it was working pretty well. Except that we were, bit by bit, gaining speed.

I panicked. I clamped too hard on the brakes, and the wheels locked. The car instantly flung out of control, spinning round and round, ricocheting off the icy walls, and then finally slamming nose first into the embankment. We were stuck, embedded too deeply to dig ourselves out.

Now what I didn't mention is the subculture, the emotional

netherworld, of most serious skiers. It is a rivalry from peak to valley. Once on the mountain, you don't have much compassion for the car troubles of your fellow man. There is no Good Samaritanism here. At the very least, when the roads are this bad, it's every man for himself. But usually there's some active spite mixed in with that. You generally feel no more pity for the man in the ditch than golfers do for the man in the bunker, in the rough, in the water; no more than hockey players do for the other team when their goon has to sit out a penalty. You're pleased and, often, not so secretly.

In short, I expected no one to help. It was dangerous anyhow. Anyone stopping would put themselves at risk: They'd either end up in the snowbank like us, or they'd put themselves in harm's way if other vehicles lost control.

So I was surprised when a few minutes later a car stopped and four brawny men jumped out and ran over. Right away, I launched into a self-justifying account of what had happened. Naturally (for me at that time), my account was thick with expletives, greasy blue clouds of cursing.

The men met this with silence. "Well," one of them said, "so much for how you got into it. Let's just get you out." They simply took matters in hand, and in a few minutes we were back on the road.

My brother started into me right away. "You idiot, do you hear yourself? Those guys were probably Christians. And your mouth was filthy as a sackful of..." Well, you get the idea.

And then our lapsed Christian friend said something I've never forgotten. "If they were Christians, it wouldn't matter to them. That's not what motivates these people. They do it for God. They do it because that's what God is like."

I was stunned into repentance. I didn't see it that way then, but that's what it was. Repentance. In that moment, I saw God's beauty. His goodness came near, near enough to touch. His name—full of mercy, abounding in compassion, slow to anger—was whispered in my ear. In four ordinary men, four simple clay jars, I caught sight of the glory of God.

WE SHOULDN'T BE SURPRISED. The most glorious thing God has ever done on earth is, in one sense, also earth's darkest thing, its ugliest, its bleakest. I'm speaking of the Cross. Here, the beauty of God and the hideousness of evil meet. Here, the God who abounds in steadfast love and yet who punishes evil comes near to us. Here, God is perfectly merciful, dying for His enemies. Here, He is being perfectly just, punishing sin without mercy.

It is His supreme glory. The night before Jesus went to the cross, He prayed, "Father, the time has come. Glorify your Son, that your Son may glorify you."[9]

The time has come. The glory of the Son, the glory of the Father, was rendered supremely in heavy cross-beams and

rough-cast metal, in hammer and spear, in bones finely splin-
tered and flesh deeply cut. *But we have this treasure in jars of
clay*. This is the all-surpassing glory of God, a derelict man,
stripped and beaten, splayed on a gibbet, His blood darken-
ing the wood, thickening around His wounds, His side
pierced so that blood and water flow out.

What does it mean to rest in this? The answer is almost
embarrassing in its simplicity. We preach Christ crucified. We
have this treasure in jars of clay. Meaning ordinary men and
women like you and me, people who mumble, trip, grieve
and laugh, get the flu, forget to floss—we take up our cross
daily and follow Him, so that a little more of the treasure spills
out, a glimmer more of the glory breaks through.

The paradox is that God's glory shines brightest in our
ordinariness, when we least strive after our usual ideas and
ideals about glory—spectacle, pageantry, victory. It shines in
our simplicity and humility, when we bring cups of cold water
to the thirsty, clothes to the naked. When we dislodge cars
from snowbanks. "I pray also," Paul wrote, "that the eyes of
your heart may be enlightened in order that you may know
the hope to which he has called you, *the riches of his glorious
inheritance in the saints.*"[10] I pray, he's saying, that you would
see beneath the clay jars of this man and that woman and see
the glory God has stashed there.

I think about people I know, the saints with their swollen
ankles or their knobby hands, the rickety prayer warriors who

don't have the physical strength to open a pickle jar but who set whole legions of demons flying for cover whenever they kneel. Some are pious misfits, holy eccentrics. Most are just ordinary, with nothing but the presence of God to distinguish them from all the other people on the face of the earth.

I think of Helen, at eighty, weighing no more than she would have as a young peasant girl escaping Stalin's Russia, spending most of her widow's pension on Bibles for Romanian orphans or AIDS victims in Angola. I think of Don, gaunt and ill-dressed as a scarecrow, looking like Mr. Bean after a hunger strike, a bachelor at fifty-five who still attends Youth Group because he loves the energy there and who spends most of his days gathering spiritual vagrants like some people collect stray cats. I think of Margaret, who prepares communion at our church. She's done this from the beginning. Sometimes she worries that her arthritis will twist and harden her hands so badly that she can no longer break the matzo bread and fill the tiny communion cups and carry the trays to the table. She is a priest in the Holy of Holies, doing her work with joy and reverence. When I watch her, I think of Anna in the temple, her entire life shaped into a prayer.

Through such as these, the whole earth is filled with God's glory.

Maybe this is hardest to believe about yourself. You can believe it for others, that in the clay jars of Helen and Don and Margaret all-surpassing treasure brims full—but not for yourself, that in your muddled, addled, unexotic life there is even the faintest stain or smallest dreg of His glory. But Paul explains that, too. Along with God's glory, he says, we also carry something else from God: "We always carry around in our body the death of Jesus, so that the life of Jesus may also be revealed in our body."[11] That's just the way of it. There is no way outside it. His glory, at its deepest, is always cruciform.

So rest in this, that when you and I are weak, He is strong. That even in our dying—especially there—He rises up. That when you break, what's inside spills out. And it is glory.

THE CHURCH, AT ITS WISEST, has always known this.

From the time of severe persecution in the early life of the church, one story stands out for me. The year was A.D. 258. The place, Rome. A deacon by the name of Laurence gave large sums of money to the poor. The Emperor Valerian, who hated Christians, had Laurence hauled into his throne room and ordered him to bring the treasures of the church or be killed. Laurence gathered a mob of poor people, crippled people, blind people, homeless people, and he brought these to the emperor. "These," Laurence said, "are the treasures of the church."[12]

One day, God will break forth in glory, and the whole

universe will not be enough to contain it. One day, all the trouble we have been dealt here will be traded for an "eternal weight of glory."[13]

But for now, God fills the whole earth with His glory one clay pot at a time.

A Took and
a Baggins

No one in my childhood home ever spoke of God. He was to us a quaint curiosity, if we thought of Him at all—an antique more rustic than exotic, something great-grandmother had, and actually used, like a washboard or a clasped watch, but which we now kept in a box under the stairs.

I went to church twice as a child, both times when I was about six. One time—the one I particularly remember—was at Easter. Even now, almost forty years gone, the memory is strong: the heavy, heady perfumes of the old ladies; the children, one of them with a coonskin hat (which awakened in me the raw power of coveting); drawing pictures of the crucifixion in Sunday school; the clicking and pinging of the heat register coming on; the soft, pallid manner of the minister greeting parishioners at the door, his hand cool and soft-boned like a dead sparrow with its feathers plucked. My mother wore a hat, like all the ladies, a snug dark pillbox like the ones Jacqueline Kennedy had made popular a few years before. I had to wear a clip-on bow tie, which I despised, and a shirt with a collar stiff as if the little wing tab of cardboard had been left in.

It was a beautiful day outside, warm and clear and the trees tinctured green with new buds—and I wondered why we had to be inside, doing something plodding and murmury, something which everyone, young and old, seemed bored with. I sat preternaturally still on the hard pew, beside a very large woman exuding a hypnotic fume of lilac and sweat, and I wondered what it would be like to live this way all the time: having to sit endlessly still, every muscle rigid from restraint; having to talk with other people in furtive whispers so low it sounded like hissing; having to pretend to be listening to the minister as his voice rose and fell, rose and fell, so that after a while you didn't hear the words at all, only the voice's contour, the way it sounded like water being poured slowly back and forth between large urns.

So at age six, having done the God thing twice and found it wanting, I quit church and did my own thing. For most of my growing-up years, I sought God as I understood Him in ways that suited me. Meaning, I only bothered with God when I was in trouble or wanted something. Later I was to find this isn't such an uncommon thing, that even the Israelites, God's chosen people, had a habit of living however they pleased—straying and defying, getting and spending—and then crying out to God when they got in too deep and needed rescue. My relationship with God was entirely like that: one-sided, self-centered, anxiety-driven. I made up the rules, dictated the terms, did as I pleased.

If all that failed, I asked God to sort it out.

And always I asked God to make me happy. He was to pluck me clean out of my predicaments and fill my cup to overflowing; but otherwise He should hover in the wings, putter in the garden shed, unobtrusive, keeping His thoughts to Himself.

Yet there was another part of me that, from earliest childhood, was aware of a different face of God: a God dangerous, wild, utterly free, who smashed the little household deities I devised and called "god," who wooed and thundered, who cared little about my happiness, who cared immensely about my joy, who hid Himself from my searching and disclosed Himself without my seeking it. Not a God who did my bidding, but who called me to surrender. Not a God who pampered, but who commanded, created, consoled. A God immensely creative and gracious and fair, but not to be trifled with, not to be presumed upon.

The Lord of the Holy Wild.

A part of me back then would rather this *not* be God. But another part hoped it was. Because my idea of God was boring.

And the more I chased my own happiness, the worse I got. At twenty-one, I came to the end of myself. I turned to God.

Now I'm a pastor, writing books, preaching sermons, greeting parishioners at the door. Sunday after Sunday, I speak to people about God. Week after week, I speak to God about people. All through, I come alongside those people, and I wait with them and search with them and listen with them. For God. This takes every bit of pluck and shrewdness I have. It exhausts me and delights me, keeps me on my toes and on my knees and sometimes, when it all catches up with me, on my back. I have discovered, as I hoped and feared in my younger days, that God is no drab pedant, meddling and puttering, but the Lion of Judah, the Lord of the Holy Wild. The God who, when He speaks or shows Himself, stirs in me two impulses at once: to run *from* Him and to run *to* Him.

I don't always understand God. I have, like Jacob, wrestled all night with Him, until I'm bone-weary, until He blesses and hobbles me. I have, like Job, sulked on my dunghill, feeling betrayed by Him, scraping my sores with potsherds. I have, like David, danced wild-limbed and ecstatic before Him, scorning the shame. I have, like Paul, felt His strength in my weakness, His death in my living, His life in my dying, His glory in my plainness. I have met God in a thousand different ways, some exhilarating as homecoming after exile, some terrifying as the phone ringing in the dead of the night.

But boring? God is as far from boring as toadstools are

from oak trees, as puddles are from oceans. As borderland is from the Holy Wild.

But if I drink from the stream, will He swallow me? And is that not what I want anyhow?

ᕼ ᕼ ᕼ

OF ALL THE BIBLE'S MANY unsettling accounts of people missing God—Pharaoh's hubris, Saul's paranoia, Haman's murderous insecurity, the prodigal's foolishness, his older brother's bitterness, Judas's betrayal, Pilate's cowardice, Herod's deadly pride—of all those stories, one haunts me most: Cain's faithlessness.

What gets me is a crisp New Testament gloss on the ancient tale. "By faith," Hebrews says, "Abel offered God a better sacrifice than Cain did."[1] Abel was a man of faith. Cain, by implication, was not.

But he was no atheist, Cain. He was no Nietzsche, rabid with blasphemy, spitting and choking on his God-hate. He was no Freud, coolly, smugly dissecting and dismissing all sacred belief as infantile cravings that adults ought to outgrow. He was not your slick and shallow work colleague, mocking and cocky in his irreligion. He was not your truck-driving neighbor, almost charming in his vulgarity, innocent in his profanity.

Cain was none of that.

Cain knew God.

Cain talked with God, maybe daily, with candor, face-to-face, as one friend talks to another. They had a relationship, God and Cain, an intimacy, even. They reasoned together. Cain complained to God, argued with Him, rebuffed Him, pleaded with Him. God rebuked Cain, invited him, questioned him, protected him.

Cain knew God.

He just had no faith.

I'm not sure how many times I'd heard this story, been upside and downside it, before I got inside it, and then it hit me: Faithlessness is not unbelief.

Faithlessness is the refusal to trust.

It's the refusal to rest in God and, therefore, risk for God.

You probably know a Cain or two. Some of them, a good many I think, are in churches, and some of them even lead churches—holding the purse strings, writing the policy, deciding the when and the how and the wherefore. Cain is the man who talks to God every day but wouldn't trust God as far as he can throw Him. He got "saved" thirty-eight years ago, but has never once worshiped. He has heard a thousand sermons and found fault with every one.

Cain is the man who would never, not for anything, not for anyone, put all his weight in God. His character will not rest in God's character. Only a fool would do that, and Cain's no fool.

He's shrewd.

I started this book—or nearly so—with a Narnia story and want to end it—or nearly so—with one. Near the close of *The Last Battle,* C. S. Lewis's seventh and final chronicle of Narnia, the hosts of Narnia fight and win a great and terrible battle against evil. Children and warriors and talking animals and King Tirian, the last of Narnia's human kings, await Aslan's appearance, excited, expectant, nervous.

But then there are the Dwarfs.

A group of Dwarfs, shrewd and suspicious, refuse to trust in all this talk of Aslan and his kingdom.

Aslan comes:

> The earth trembled. The sweet air grew suddenly sweeter. A brightness flashed behind them. All turned. Tirian turned last because he was afraid. There stood his heart's desire, huge and real, the golden Lion, Aslan himself, and already the others were kneeling in a circle around his forepaws and burying their hands and faces in his mane as he stooped his great head to touch them with his tongue. Then he fixed his eyes upon Tirian, and Tirian came near, trembling, and flung himself at the Lion's feet, and the Lion kissed him and said, "Well done, last of the Kings of Narnia who stood firm at the darkest hour."

But then there are the Dwarfs.

Lucy pleads with Aslan, "Could you—will you—do something for these poor Dwarfs?"

"Dearest," says Aslan, "I will show you both what I can, and what I cannot, do."

No matter what Aslan does—stand in the very midst of the Dwarfs, growl at them, provide a sumptuous feast for them—they won't trust. "We haven't let anyone take us in," they proudly declare. "The Dwarfs are for the Dwarfs."

> "You see," said Aslan, "They will not let us help them. They have chosen cunning instead of belief. Their prison is only in their own minds, yet they are in that prison; and so afraid of being taken in that they cannot be taken out. But come, children. I have other work to do."[2]

The Dwarfs are for the Dwarfs.

Cain is for Cain.

So afraid of being taken in, they can't be taken out.

And though the Holy Wild might be a hairbreadth away, as close as your brother Abel, it may as well be a whole world removed.

ϡ ϡ ϡ

AS I WAS WRITING THIS BOOK, Cheryl was reading *The Hobbit* to our daughters, Sarah and Nicola. Most evenings, after the girls had bathed and slipped into their nighties, they would sit on either side of their mother, munching quartered apples, and Cheryl would open the book to the place where they'd left off, and their eyes would grow wide and round and bright. Cheryl's voice danced—growing tight with dread or airy with mirth or raspy and urgent with suspense—with J. R. R. Tolkien's swiftly tilting prose.

It's the story, if you don't know it, of twelve dwarfs who, under the sporadic direction of Gandalf the wizard and the despotic leadership of Thorin Oakenshield, the head dwarf, recruit the hobbit Bilbo Baggins and head off on a long journey to rob a dragon's lair. Bilbo is their "thief," the one appointed, without any say in the matter, to outwit Smaug the dragon and loot his sprawling hoard of treasure.

It is an odyssey of windfalls and pitfalls, tight scrapes and narrow escapes, danger and wonder all the way. It's an escapade. They meet elves and trolls, giants and goblins, spiders as big as ponies, wolves that talk, a man who turns into a bear, eagles so strong they can pluck up and carry grown men in their talons. They slither down caves, scramble through forests, run headlong across fields, hide in wine kegs. They tell riddles and solve them. It's a journey of luck and pluck and skin-of-their-teeth exploits, of wrong turns turned shortcuts, of accidents that save the day. Along the way, their backsides toughen and their hearts soften, and—slow, slow, slow—folly gives way to wisdom. The journey changes them, all of them, forever.[3]

Bilbo, the hobbit, never wanted to go. Or he did. That's the thing. Bilbo is a Baggins, and Bagginses love comfort, protection, routine. They have no higher ambition than to be home for dinner on time and to get a good night's sleep. They're bereft of wanderlust. They just want to curl up snug in their own thick shadows and never venture out much past the local pub. Anything more is perilous and foolhardy.

But Bilbo has Took blood in him, too. The Tooks are a different sort of creature: curious, restless, a bit wild. The more sedentary, quiet-loving hobbits regard them with suspicion. They're strange folk, quixotic, not altogether there. The Tooks have an appetite for danger, a hunger for adventure, a craving for discovery. They abound in wanderlust. They want to cast long shadows and strike out over the horizon. Anything less is safe and boring.

In Bilbo, the Baggins blood and the Took blood mix and war. The Baggins in him shrinks from menace and disruption; the Took in him longs for it. The Baggins bones cling to comfort; the Took blood chafes beneath it. In the end, Took wins out and the result is unforgettable, a timeless story that makes my daughters' eyes bright with wonder, my wife's voice a thing of magic.

I'm a Baggins.

I'm also a Took.

A part of me would rather stay right here, tucked up in the drab safeness of routine, knowing always where the next meal is coming from, what it will be, when it's ready.

But another part itches to go plunder a dragon's hoard, come what may.

Jesus invites us to know God, know Him in all His beauty and terror, His brusqueness and tenderness, His wooing and commanding. And the invitation is both to rest in Him *and* to risk for Him. To come. To go.

To be a Took and a Baggins both.

It's an invitation to the Holy Wild, where all who are weary can find rest for their souls—and all who are bored can go holy swashbuckling. There's bread to spare and dragons to slay.

And if you're tired, go ahead, lay down and sleep.

There are no serpents hidden beneath the bed that He can't deal with.

NOTES

Chapter One

1. Eugene Peterson used this phrase as the title of a book, but it originates with the German philosopher Friedrich Nietzsche.

2. C. S. Lewis, *The Silver Chair* (Middlesex, England: Puffin Books, 1977), 26–7.

3. A. W. Tozer, *The Knowledge of the Holy* (New York: Harper & Row, 1961), 1.

4. RBC Ministries, "Beyond Our Understanding," *Our Daily Bread* (11 June 1995).

5. Luke 4:34, my emphasis.

6. Luke 8:28, my emphasis.

7. Acts 16:17, my emphasis.

8. James 2:19.

9. *The Lord of the Rings: The Fellowship of the Ring,* based on the book by J. R. R. Tolkien, a New Line Cinema and Wingnut Films Production, 2001.

Chapter Two

1. Habakkuk 1:2–7, 9, 11.

2. Habakkuk 1:13.

3. Ruth A. Tucker, *Walking Away from Faith: Unraveling the Mystery of Belief and Unbelief* (Downer's Grove, IL: InterVarsity Press, 2002), 15.

4. See Habakkuk 2:7–17.

5. Habakkuk 2:4.

6. 2 Samuel 18:33.

7. Justine Berkhiem, "A Mother's Dreams Are in the Father's Hands," unpublished poem—until now, Justine! Bless you and thank you.

Chapter Three

1. Philip Yancey, "What Surprised Jesus," *Christianity Today*, 12 September 1994, 88.

2. J. Allan Petersen, *The Myth of the Greener Grass* (Wheaton, IL: Tyndale, 1992), 17.

3. Acts 17:28.

4. See Exodus 34:6; Deuteronomy 32:4; 2 Samuel 22:26; Psalm 33:4; 36:5; 57:3; 61:7; 89:8, 14, 33; 91:4; 117:2; 119:75; 145:13; Lamentations 3:23; Romans 3:3; 1 Corinthians 10:13; 1 Thessalonians 5:24; 2 Thessalonians 3:3; 1 John 1:9; Revelation 3:14; 19:11.

5. See Genesis 15:17.

6. Hebrews 6:13, 17–19.

7. I wrote about this in my first book, *Your God Is Too Safe* (Sisters, OR: Multnomah Publishers), 72–3.

8. See 1 Kings 17:1–6; 19:1–18.

9. 2 Corinthians 1:8–9.

10. 2 Corinthians 11:23–28.

11. 2 Corinthians 1:9–10, my emphasis.

12. See 2 Corinthians 12:7–10.

13. Hebrews 11:36–38; 12:1–3.

14. See James 1:2.

15. Personal e-mail from John Polus, November 6, 2002.

16. 1 John 1:9.

17. 1 Thessalonians 5:23–24, my emphasis.

18. Luke 10:20, my emphasis.

Chapter Four

1. William Shakespeare, *King Lear,* 4.1, spoken by the Earl of Gloucester.

2. Cornelius Tacitus, *The Annals,* Book XV, chapter 44.

3. Cited in Bill Moyer, *Genesis: A Living Conversation* (New York: Doubleday, 1996), 62.

4. See 1 John 4:8.

5. 1 John 3:1.

6. 1 John 4:9–10.

7. Dennis Ngien, "The God Who Suffers," *Christianity Today,* 3 February 1997, 40.

8. See John 13:17.

9. 1 John 4:11–12, my emphasis.

10. 1 John 4:16, my emphasis.

11. I have lost my source for this story.

12. 1 Corinthians 13:1–8.

13. Robert Munsch, illustrated by Sheila McGraw, *Love You Forever* (Toronto: Firefly Books, 1986).

14. Zephaniah 3:16–17.

Chapter Five

1. Romans 1:18–24, 26, 28.

2. Nicholas Dawidoff, *In the Country of Country: People and Places in American Music* (New York: Pantheon Books, 1997), cited in Rodney Clapp, "From Holiness to Honky-Tonks: Race and Religion in Country Music," *Books & Culture,* September/October 1997, 9.

3. "Rabbi Say Wig-Wearing Women Burn in Hell," *Jerusalem Post* (AP), 1998.

4. Matthew 10:28.

5. See John 3:16.

6. John 3:19–20.

7. Proverbs 29:11.

8. Galatians 5:20.

9. James 1:20.

10. Romans 1:32, *The Message.*

11. C. S. Lewis, *The Problem of Pain* (New York: MacMillan, 1947), 115–6.

12. Hebrews 12:5–6; see also Proverbs 3:11–12.

13. Romans 1:18–21.

14. Hebrews 12:15.

15. Romans 3:9.

16. Romans 5:8–9.

17. 1 Thessalonians 1:10.

Chapter Six

1. Luke 10:25–29.
2. Luke 10:36–37.
3. Romans 11:32, my emphasis.
4. Ephesians 2:4–5, my emphasis.
5. 1 Timothy 1:15–16, my emphasis.
6. 2 Samuel 24–3.
7. 2 Samuel 24:10.
8. 2 Samuel 24:11–13.
9. 2 Samuel 24:14, my emphasis.
10. 1 Peter 1:3–4.

Chapter Seven

1. Matthew 28:18; Revelation 5:6.
2. *The Mission*, a Warner Bros./Goldcrest and Kingsmere Production, 1986.
3. Colossians 2:15.
4. Acts 17:6, AMP.
5. Romans 8:37.
6. See Judges 6:1–7:25.
7. 1 John 3:8.
8. Revelation 12:11.
9. A brief capsule of the story is found in Kenneth Scott Latourette's *A History of Christianity, Volume 1: Beginnings to 1500* (New York: Harper & Row, 1975), 245. Or see chapter 3 of *Fox's Book of Martyrs*, available on-line at the Christian Classics Ethereal Library.

http://www.ccel.org/f/foxe_j/martyrs/fox103.htm
(accessed 25 June 2003).

10. Romans 8:31–39.

11. Mark A. Noll, *A History of Christianity in the United States and Canada* (Grand Rapids, MI: Eerdmans Publishing, 1992), 544.

Chapter Eight

1. Isaiah 6:1–9.

2. See 2 Chronicles 26.

3. "The Business of Making Saints: An Interview with Eugene Peterson," *Leadership Journal*, Spring 1997, 22.

4. See Revelation 4:8.

5. *Kadesh* in Hebrew, *hagio* in Greek.

6. Leviticus 11:44–45, cited in 1 Peter 1:16.

7. See Mark 2:1–12.

8. 1 John 1:7.

9. T. S. Eliot, "Little Gidding," *The Four Quartets*, section 4, lines 204–6, 212–3.

10. *The Mission*, a Warner Bros./Goldcrest and Kingsmere Production, 1986.

11. Anne Lamott, *Traveling Mercies: Some Thoughts on Faith* (New York: Anchor Books, 1999), 63–5.

12. Revelation 4:2–3, 6, 8; 5:11–13.

13. Revelation 5:6.

14. John 1:29.

Chapter Nine

1. Sandra Vida, "The Power of the Spoken Word: Michael St. George," *FFWD*, 27 March 2003. http://www.greatwest.ca/ffwd/Issues/2003/0327/mus1.htm (accessed 25 June 2003).

2. Proverbs 25:2.

3. Isaiah 45:15.

4. Job 40:15–24, *The Message*.

5. Job 40:4–5; 42:3, 5–6, *The Message*.

Chapter Ten

1. "There Ought to Be a Law," *Vancouver Sun*, July 1997.

2. Paul M. Johnson, *Intellectuals* (London: Weidenfeld and Nicolson, 1988).

3. Romans 1:21–22, my emphasis.

4. See Matthew 16:15–23.

5. Romans 16:27, my emphasis.

6. Douglas Groothuis, "Jesus the Philosopher," *Books & Culture*, January/February 2003, 38.

7. See 1 Corinthians 1:23–24.

8. See Matthew 11:25.

9. Proverbs 3:19–20.

10. Wilbur Nelson, *If I Were an Atheist* (Grand Rapids, MI: Baker, 1973), cited in *Our Daily Bread*, 6 August 1994.

11. Ephesians 3:10.

12. Charles Colson, *The Body* (Nashville: Word Publishing, 1992), 11ff.

13. See 1 Corinthians 1:26.

14. 1 Corinthians 1:28, 30.

15. 1 Corinthians 1:20.

16. 1 Corinthians 1:18.

17. Acts 17:18.

18. See 1 Kings 3:16–28.

Chapter Eleven

1. *Cast Away*, an ImageMovers/Playtone Production, distributed by 20th Century Fox and DreamWorks, 2000.

2. Numbers 15:32–36.

3. Wayne Muller, *Sabbath: Finding Rest, Renewal, and Delight in Our Busy Lives* (New York: Bantam Books, 1999), 82–3.

4. Exodus 20:8–11.

5. RBC Ministries, "Let's Go Fishing!" *Our Daily Bread* (18 May 1996).

6. Mark 2:27.

7. Isaiah 58:13–14.

8. Cited in Muller, *Sabbath*, 190.

9. Genesis 2:21–22.

10. Muller, *Sabbath*, 151.

Chapter Twelve

1. Exodus 33:12–17.

2. Exodus 33:19.

3. Exodus 34:5–7.

4. 2 Corinthians 3:7–11.

5. 2 Corinthians 3:12–18.

6. 2 Corinthians 4:6.

7. 2 Corinthians 4:1–6.

8. 2 Corinthians 4:7.

9. John 17:2.

10. Ephesians 1:18, my emphasis.

11. 2 Corinthians 4:10.

12. James R. Edwards, "At the Crossroads," *Christianity Today,* 11 August 1997, 25.

13. 2 Corinthians 4:17, NKJV.

Epilogue

1. Hebrews 11:4.

2. C. S. Lewis, *The Last Battle* (Middlesex, England: Puffin Books, 1978), 134–5.

3. J. R. R. Tolkien, *The Hobbit: Or There and Back Again* (Boston: Houghton Mifflin, 1999).

Do You Love God from a Safe Distance?

"I'm convinced Mark Buchanan is a rising talent in Christian writing. His writing always leaves me moved, stimulated, and convicted. I find myself mulling it over days later and wishing for more."

—PHILIP YANCEY

Here's a thoughtful, probing exploration of why Christians get stuck in the place of complacency, dryness, and tedium—and how to move on to new levels of spiritual passion! Buchanan shows how the majority of Christians begin their spiritual journey with excitement and enthusiasm—only to get bogged down in a "borderland"—an in-between space beyond the "old life" but short of the abundant, adventurous existence promised by Jesus. Citing Jonah, Buchanan examines the problem of "borderland living"—where doubt, disappointment, guilt, and wonderlessness keep people in a quagmire of mediocrity—then offers solutions… effective ways to get unstuck and move into a bold, unpredictable, exhilarating walk with Christ. Inspired writing!

ISBN 1-57673-774-8

LIVING IN LIGHT OF FOREVER

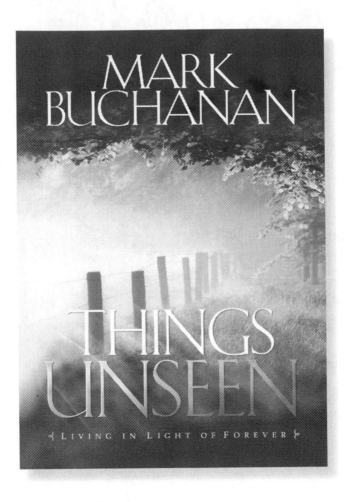

Blending pastoral warmth, philosophical depth, storytelling skill, and literary craft, Mark Buchanan encourages Christians to make heaven, literally, our "fixation"—filling our vision, gripping our heart, and anchoring our hope. Only then, says Buchanan, can we become truly fearless on this earth, free from the fear of losing our life, property, status, title, or comfort; free from the threat of tyrants, the power of armies, and the day of trouble. Buchanan reawakens the instinctive yearning for things above, showing that only the heavenly minded are of much earthly good.

ISBN 1-57673-889-2

Printed in the United States
by Baker & Taylor Publisher Services